When Catholics Die

Eternal Life
or
Eternal Damnation?

All Scripture references are quoted from the King James translation of the Holy Bible, unless otherwise noted.

When Catholics Die
Copyright ©1999 by Dick Noll
Revised & Reprinted 2001
Published by The Olive Press, a division of Midnight Call Ministries
Columbia, SC 29228 U.S.A.

    Copy typist: Lynn Jeffcoat
    Copy editor: Susanna Cancassi
   Proofreaders: Angie Peters, Susanna Cancassi
   Lithography: Simon Froese, Ryan Guerra
Cover Design: J Spurling

Library of Congress Cataloging-in-Publication Data

   When Catholics Die
   ISBN# 0-937422-46-0

Printed in the United States of America

This book is dedicated to my loving and devoted wife of 41 years, Lee Noll, always a source of boundless encouragement. Also to Joni Coons and Jerri Graves who pulled me through my early struggles with authorship.

FOREWORD BY ARNO FROESE

Rarely have I read a story as amazing as that of this Catholic, Dick Noll, who broke through to a living faith in the Lord Jesus Christ.

Dissatisfied with the "status quo," he has diligently worked to uncover teachings which are contrary to the Scripture and which even contradict the Statement of Faith of the Catholic Church as set forth in the Catechism.

Dick Noll has done an excellent job of analyzing the discrepancies between biblical doctrine and doctrine that originated with the tradition of man.

Catholics and non-Catholics alike will greatly benefit from the information in this book, *When Catholics Die*, which has personally given me a deeper insight into scriptural facts which often are "traditionalized away" by man's word.

Unfortunately, this tendency is not found exclusively in the Catholic Church, but it seems prevalent in virtually all denominations. One could rightly ask, "What will happen when Baptists die? When Presbyterians die? When Lutherans die? When Pentecostals die?"

The answer can obviously be only one of two: Either they are saved through grace on the merits of the shed blood of Christ or they are lost for all eternity, deceived by the traditions of man.

I have read this book several times and no doubt will read it again, each time benefitting from Dick Noll's remarkable ability to compare the Word of God with the word of man. ■

When Catholics Die
Vatican Doctrine
The Precepts of Men vs. The Bible, The Word of God
A Common Sense Approach to Discerning the Truth

By Richard A. Noll

TABLE OF CONTENTS

ABOUT THE AUTHOR

Raised as a dedicated Catholic, Richard A. Noll, according to his family, seemed destined to become a Catholic priest. As a child, he often served at as many as three early morning masses before attending Catholic grammar school classes.

Noll graduated from a Catholic high school and completed his formal education at Pace College in New York City.

For 64 years he faithfully attended Sunday Mass, estimating he missed no more than two dozen times.

In 1955 he convinced his fiancé, Leona "Lee" Bogordos, to convert to Catholicism. Forty-one years of an exceptionally happy marriage brought the blessings of four children and four equally wonderful grandchildren. Lee died in 1996 after a long battle with cancer.

During the year prior to Lee's death, the Noll's left the Catholic Church and joined a Bible-believing congregation.

Between 1980 and 1995, the author continued to attend Sunday Mass solely due to his wife's wishes.

After her initial diagnosis of cancer, four different oncologists predicted she would live only a few years, but the Lord kept her alive for eleven years, the exact amount of time necessary for her to recognize the truth of God's Word.

With new enthusiasm and vigor, she accepted Jesus Christ's death at Calvary as the exclusive reason for her salvation. Shortly thereafter, the Lord took His beloved child and the author's beloved wife home to be with Him forever!

The author, who had made this same commitment to Christ 15 years earlier, had also become an ardent and enthusiastic student of God's Word, the Holy Bible.

That eternally important turning point in his own life prompted Richard to seek the help of many Bible scholars. The commentators he most frequently refers to are in virtual unity in their understanding and teaching of an inerrant Bible. They include: Dave Hunt, Arno Froese, Chuck Missler, Dr. David Reagan, Dr. David Breese, Dr. John MacArthur, J.R. Church, Dr. Charles Stanley, Dr. David Webber, Dr. Ed Vallowe, Moody Adams, Dr. John Ankerberg, Peter Lalonde, Hal Lindsey, Mike Gendron, Dr. John Walvoord, Dr. J. Dwight Pentecost, and Dr. D. James Kennedy.

PREFACE

Outside the [Roman] Catholic Church there is no salvation. Basing itself on Scripture and Tradition, the Council teaches that the Church, a pilgrim now on earth, is necessary for salvation: the one Christ is the mediator and the way of salvation; he is present to us in his body which is the Church. He himself explicitly asserted the necessity of faith and Baptism, and thereby affirmed at the same time the necessity of the Church which men enter through Baptism as through a door. Hence they could not be saved who, knowing that the Catholic Church was founded as necessary by God through Christ, would refuse either to enter it or to remain in it.

Catechism of the Catholic Church - 846

"Neither is there salvation in any other: for there is none other name under heaven given among men, whereby we must be saved."

Acts 4:12

Recently the Vatican indicated that its latest census counted one billion Catholics world-wide. Some are very dedicated in their faith and others are Catholics in name only. Most are probably somewhere in between. Few, however, are aware of the vast irreconcilable differences that exist between what the Bible teaches and what the Vatican teaches. This leads us to the central theme of this book, *When Catholics Die*: What happens?

If the Bible is right and the Vatican wrong, then the potential outlook for Catholics is eternal damnation!

Strong and scary words, yes! But I can assure the Catholic reader of four things:

• First, if you undertake your own thorough investigation, you will discover that the Bible is the Holy Spirit-inspired Word of God. The Catholic Church confirms this in the new (1994) Catechism.

• Second, and in direct contradiction to the above, the majority of what modern Catholicism teaches is the creation of mortal men, not inspired by the Holy Spirit. The Vatican labels this teaching as "Catholic Tradition."

• Third, you will realize that the Bible is the complete counsel of God, nothing is to be added to or subtracted from it (Revelation 22:18–19).

• Fourth, once you recognize that truth, it must follow that Catholic Tradition deceives its followers because it is an addendum to Scripture; virtually all of it is unbiblical.

In referring to the eternal disposition of Catholics, I have throughout this text carefully inserted the word "potential" because there is still time for each Catholic to determine the truth on his or her own. And therein lies the objective of this book.

I have invested a large portion of my time during the past 17 years doing what I am asking you to do: Initiate your own unbiased research. If you do, this book may be the best place to start.

Allow me to provide a flying start toward answering the question, "Have we been deceived by Catholic Tradition?"

My goal is to convince you of a profound truth: You need only the sufficiency contained in God's Word to be saved. Suffering under the bondage of Catholic Tradition and certain other Catholic doctrine contributes nothing toward our salvation.

You may become incredulous when reading the new (1994) *Catechism of the Catholic Church*. The portions pertaining to the validity of Holy Scripture justify what Protestant reformers such as Luther, Calvin, Knox and Wesley tried to establish. Because of their beliefs, which are now similar to portions of the Catechism, they were anathematized, or cursed, by Vatican Councils.

"The Council of Trent pronounced the anathema more than 100 times upon those who accepted the beliefs of the Reformers; Vatican II reconfirmed those anathemas and added one of its own; and thus Roman Catholicism damns to eternal hell all evangelical Christians today." [1]

History relates that multitudes of Christians have been killed under the direct orders of popes because of their biblical beliefs and their refusal to conform to Vatican teaching. Thus, we should be overwhelmed when pondering the Vatican's endorsement of scriptural inerrancy because the doctrine of scriptural inerrancy lays waste to virtually all Catholic Tradition and most other Catholic doctrine. These conflicting declarations by the Church of Rome confuse us all. Accordingly, the first chapter of this book establishes the Vatican's endorsement of the inerrancy of Holy Scripture.

This confusion demands that a large portion of this book illustrate how Catholic Tradition conflicts with its own Catechism's teaching of scriptural inerrancy. Another, but shorter, section of this book will describe the sordid history of the Church of Rome. By looking at its past, we can get a good grip on the character of its current condition.

Little has changed in recent years except the Vatican's need for modern public relations, imaging, and communications.

Obviously, some parts of this book may be quite difficult for Catholics to digest. Had I read it myself during my many years as a faithful and zealous Catholic, it would have deeply upset me. You may even sympathize with my own need to admit that I had been deceived for such a long time.

Catholic readers will make their own decisions as to the validity of their church's doctrine. Some may recognize a certain and perhaps unique advantage of reading a book about Catholic beliefs that is not authored by a theologian. Rather, it is written by a longtime Catholic layman who has strong empathy for the Catholic reader.

I discovered during my long and arduous search for the truth that I was dealing with an issue requiring a lot of common sense. If you apply a large measure of that ingredient to your analysis of my arguments, you will assuredly discern the truth. Like me, you, my Catholic brother or sister, may have been deceived.

[1]Dave Hunt, *A Woman Rides The Beast*, Harvest House Publishers, 1994, p. 521.

Chapter 1

Validity of Holy Scripture Teachings: Excerpts From *The Catechism of the Catholic Church* (1994)

The inspired books teach the truth. "Since therefore all that the inspired authors or sacred writers affirm should be regarded as affirmed by the Holy Spirit, we must acknowledge that the books of Scripture firmly, faithfully, and without error teach that truth which God, for the sake of our salvation, wished to see confided to the Sacred Scriptures.

Catechism of the Catholic Church - 107

"All scripture is given by inspiration of God, and is profitable for doctrine, for reproof, for correction, for instruction in righteousness."

2ⁿᵈ Timothy 3:16

This book will make a great deal of sense if you understand the following elements of the Catechism when reading the Scripture quotations contained throughout its chapters.

> *God is the author of sacred Scripture*: "The divinely revealed realities, which are contained and presented in the text of Sacred Scripture, have been written down under the inspiration of the Holy Spirit" (P.31: #105).

> God inspired the human authors of the sacred books. "To compose the sacred books, God chose certain men who, all the while he employed them in this task, made full use of their own facilities and powers so that, though he acted in them and by them, it was as true authors that they consigned to writing whatever he wanted written, and no more" (p.31 #106).

> The inspired books teach the truth. "Since therefore all that the inspired authors or sacred writers affirm should be regarded as affirmed by the Holy Spirit, we must acknowledge that the books of Scripture firmly, faithfully, and without error teach that truth which God, for the sake of our salvation, wished to see confided to the Sacred Scriptures" (p.31: #107).

> "*Sacred Scripture* is the speech of God as it is put down in writing under the breath of the Holy Spirit." (p.26: #81).

> God is the author of sacred Scripture because he inspired its human authors; he acts in them and by means of them. He thus gives assurance that their writings teach without error his saving truth (p.37: #136).

"Faith is first of all a personal adherence of man to God. At the same time, and inseparably, it is a *free assent to the whole truth that God has revealed.* As personal adherence to God and assent to his truth, Christian faith differs from our faith in any human person. It is right and just to entrust oneself wholly to God and to believe absolutely what he says. It would be futile and false to place such faith in a creature" (p.40–41: #150).

It is of vital importance for us to establish all of the above firmly in our minds because throughout this book we will underscore that the Catholic Church hierarchy could not possibly believe these teachings. Over the centuries, it has created "infallible" doctrine diametrically opposed to the Bible and even to the Catechism that was completed in 1994.

Always keep in mind that the Catechism claims that Scripture is inerrant (#107 & #136) and that we should not place faith in the word of man, but only in the Word of God (#150). Further, note that the Catechism states that God consigned to the authors of Scripture what He wanted written and no more (#106).

Chapter 2

Sufficiency of the Living Word

"*Sacred Scripture* is the speech of God as it is put down in writing under the breath of the Holy Spirit." "And [Holy] *Tradition* transmits in its entirety the Word of God which has been entrusted to the apostles by Christ the Lord and the Holy Spirit. It transmits it to the successors of the apostles so that, enlightened by the Spirit of truth, they may faithfully preserve, expound, and spread it abroad by their preaching." As a result the Church, to whom the transmission and interpretation of Revelation is entrusted, "does not derive her certainty about all revealed truths from the holy Scriptures alone. Both Scripture and Tradition must be accepted and honored with equal sentiments of devotion and reverence."

The Catechism of the Catholic Church - 81, 82

"*Beware lest any man spoil you through philosophy and vain deceit, after the tradition of men, after the rudiments of the world, and not after Christ.*"

Colossians 2:8

My 64 years among the Catholic faithful has convinced me that most believe in the creation of the universe as described in the first sentence of the Bible: *"In the beginning God created the heaven and the earth"* (Genesis 1:1).

Also, most believe in the biblical account of the creation of mankind: *"And God said, Let us make man in our image, after our likeness..."* (Genesis 1:26).

"And the LORD God formed man of the dust of the ground, and breathed into his nostrils the breath of life; and man became a living soul" (Genesis 2:7).

But who is this *"our"* of the phrase, *"our likeness"*? The answer is found in the book of John: *"In the beginning was the Word, and the Word was with God, and the Word was God. The same was in the beginning with God"* (John 1:1–2).

Jesus Christ, who is the Word, was with His Father and He was the Creator. *"All things were made by him; and without him was not any thing made that was made"* (John 1:3).

But there is something else very important we should know about the "Word." In the Greek, "word" is "logos," which means "an expression of thought." The entirety of Holy Scripture is God's expression, His thoughts, and His commands which He expects mankind to unquestionably obey. It's our instruction book from the Creator.

If He has the power to create all things, including mankind, He certainly has the power to provide us with His inerrant instructions.

Sometimes we overlook just how aweseome Jesus Christ's creation really is. So let's devote a little time to exploring His incredible handiwork. Perhaps then we can better comprehend the magnitude of this, and therefore more easily understand the Creator's ability to provide us with His inviolable Book of instructions.

Scientists generally agree that the known totality of creation spans a breadth of 60 billion light years.

Most of us remember from our high school science class that light travels at the rate of 186,000 miles per second. Multiply 186,000 x 60 x 60 x 24 x 365 to establish the distance light travels in one year. The resulting number must be multiplied by 60 billion to determine the fullness of the currently perceived universe.

And so, Jesus Christ, who always was and always is, along with God the Father and the Holy Spirit, created everything. Not just everything in the physical realm, but everything in the spiritual realm as well — the means for us to be with Him forever in eternity as expressed in His written Word. He is the Word, the entirety of Scripture which contains the full and only instruction necessary to insure salvation. Everything else as it relates to our salvation is superfluous.

It's a great mystery, then, why the Catholic Catechism also proclaims that Holy Scripture is inerrant and that nothing should be added to it. This contradicts Catholic Tradition, which teaches that we are saved by faith *plus* works — the *opposite* of the Bible's clear teaching that our works add nothing to our salvation:

"For by grace are ye saved through faith; and that not of yourselves: it is the gift of God: Not of works, lest any man should boast" (Ephesians 2:8–9).

The Church of Rome teaches that salvation comes through faith, plus works, (i.e., participation in the church sacraments, including transubstantiation during Mass, through indulgences, purgatory, through Mary, usage of the confessional, and many other unbiblical doctrines).

In fact, the entire Catholic organizational structure — nuns, priests, bishops, cardinals, the pope, etc. — is nowhere to be found in Scripture.

The only exception is that the Bible does mention another kind of priest. In the Old Testament, the tribe of Levi provided priests who presided over temple worship and sacrifice.

The advent of the Gospel of Jesus Christ abolished that particular need for believers under the New Covenant, which covers all who believe in salvation exclusively through the shed blood of Jesus Christ. These believers are called *"...kings and priests..."* in Revelation 1:6.

Historians point out that most all of the early Church Fathers believed in the shed blood of Jesus Christ as the exclusive means of salvation. The term "Church Fathers" is the designation historians use when referring to the early church leadership, those who immediately followed in the steps of Christ's apostles and disciples.

"In whom we have redemption through his blood, the forgiveness of sins, according to the riches of his grace" (Ephesians 1:7).

"Much more then, being now justified by his blood, we shall be saved from wrath through him" (Romans 5:9).

"But if we walk in the light, as he is in the light, we have fellowship one with another, and the blood of Jesus Christ his Son cleanseth us from all sin" (1st John 1:7).

Note that Jesus' blood *"cleanseth us from all sin."* This is not a partial cleansing, but a total cleansing! Theological concepts and inventions of man-made and imposed doctrine, whether labeled Catholic Tradition or anything else, are an abomination to God the Father, the Son and the Holy Spirit.

Not until 400 years after Christ's death was purely Catholic doctrine developed and declared as equal to the Word of God.

This is not to suggest that the early Christian Church was free from heresies up until that time. Certainly not; in fact,

immediately following its inception, the Church was belea-
guered by those offering their own interpretations and
addendums to God's Word. Approximately 67 years following Christ's death, the apostle Peter wrote,

*"But there were false prophets also among the people,
even as there shall be false teachers among you, who priv-
ily shall bring in damnable heresies, even denying the Lord
that bought them, and bring upon themselves swift
destruction. And many shall follow their pernicious ways;
by reason of whom the way of truth shall be evil spoken of.
And through covetousness shall they with feigned words
make merchandise of you: whose judgment now of a long
time lingereth not, and their damnation slumbereth not"*
(2nd Peter 2:1–3).

Common sense, however, leads us to believe that
Christians were saved by believing solely in the Scriptures
for hundreds of years before the advent of Catholic
Tradition, the precepts of men.

The book of 2nd Timothy, written in approximately
A.D. 66–67, clearly assures us that knowledge of
Scripture alone is always sufficient for salvation, even
when true believers in the Gospel of Jesus Christ are
besieged by false teaching.

*"But evil men and seducers shall wax worse and worse,
deceiving, and being deceived. But continue thou in the
things which thou hast learned and hast been assured of,
knowing of whom thou hast learned them; And that from a
child thou hast known the holy scriptures, which are able
to make thee wise unto salvation through faith which is in
Christ Jesus"* (2nd Timothy 3:13–15).

Indeed, the impostors did proceed from bad to worse.
Men were proclaiming that their own doctrine, inspired by
their own imagination, became equal in authority to the doctrine of God inspired by the Holy Spirit.

The Vatican was now labeling the new doctrines and precepts as the "Tradition of the Catholic Church." All Catholic Tradition, when carefully viewed in the light of God's Word, appears to be blatant deception because Jesus Christ has a profound disdain for the precepts of men.

When lecturing the Pharisees, the elite Jewish religious leaders, and some of the scribes, Jesus quoted from the Old Testament:

"He answered and said unto them, Well hath Esaias prophesied of you hypocrites, as it is written, This people honoureth me with their lips, but their heart is far from me. Howbeit in vain do they worship me, teaching for doctrines the commandments of men. For laying aside the commandment of God, ye hold the tradition of men, as the washing of pots and cups: and many other such like things ye do. And he said unto them, Full well ye reject the commandment of God, that ye may keep your own tradition" (Mark 7:6–9).

The Holy Spirit saw to it that these words were placed into both the Old and New Testaments. This signals a strong and direct testimony from Jesus Christ about the importance of His Word and the unmistakable meaning of His message.

These words also perfectly describe the underlying characteristics of the church of Rome; past, present, and future: *"...This people honoureth me with their lips, but their heart is far from me"* (Mark 7:6).

You may well ask the question, "How can anyone use the word 'future' when relating to the character of the Catholic Church?" This is one time in which the future can be accurately predicted because the Bible prophesies about endtime events.

Many Bible students from the very beginning have identified the role of the Catholic Church in the years ahead. If you spend enough time studying the Bible, particularly the book of Revelation, you, too, may recognize the role of the Catholic Church; past, present, and future. You may begin to realize that the Bible identifies the Catholic Church as playing a major role in the times in which we are now living.

Ask God the Father, in Jesus' name, for guidance and for the Holy Spirit to implant in you a love for reading His precious Word. Also ask for the ability to discern the truth of His Word. I can assure you, if you approach this with humility and sincerity, your prayer will be answered.

Chapter 3

Your Salvation Assured

Holy Baptism is the basis of the whole Christian life, the gateway to life in the Spirit (*vitae spiritualis ianua*), and the door which gives access to the other sacraments. Through Baptism we are freed from sin and reborn as sons of God; we become members of Christ, are incorporated into the Church and made sharers in her mission: "Baptism is the sacrament of regeneration through water in the word."

The Catechism of the Catholic Church - 1213

Since Baptism signifies liberation from sin and from its instigator the devil, one or more *exorcisms* are pronounced over the candidate. The celebrant then anoints him with the oil of catechumens, or lays his hands on him, and he explicitly renounces Satan. Thus prepared, he is able to *confess the faith of the Church*, to which he will be "entrusted" by Baptism.

The Catechism of the Catholic Church - 1237

"For by grace are ye saved through faith; and that not of yourselves: it is the gift of God: Not of works, lest any man should boast."

Ephesians 2:8-9

One of the all-time great preachers of the Word of God was Billy Sunday.

A friend found a tract from a 1922 Billy Sunday revival meeting in her grandmother's Bible. This tract illustrates that when dealing with biblical truths, things that were true and accurate in 1922 are still true and accurate today.

Unlike the precepts of men, which can change and contradict subsequent precepts, the Word of God never changes.

Billy Sunday's tract presented, "What It Means To Be A Christian" and described a true Christian as:

> "...any man, woman or child who comes to God as a lost sinner, accepts the Lord Jesus Christ as his personal Savior, surrenders to Him as his Lord and Master, confesses Him as such before the world, and strives to please Him in everything day by day."

If you want to be saved and be with the Savior for all eternity rather than be denied this glorious gift, then you must ask yourself the following questions:

• Have you come to God in prayer confessing that you are a lost sinner?

• Have you accepted Jesus Christ as your personal Savior and Lord of your life?

• Do you believe with total conviction that God the Father laid all of your iniquity on His Son because of your own inability to pay the price for your sins?

You must believe that you are forgiven because Jesus died for your sins and there is nothing you can do to help pay this penalty. Nothing! No sacraments, indulgences, or a stay in purgatory will save your soul!

You must leave behind the notion and the fictitious asserstion by the Catholic Church that Jesus' shed blood was insufficient and that you need to do something to help Him. You can no longer think this way because His Word consistently repeats that He alone is sufficient for salvation.

Because of this conviction, you should have the desire to tell the world about this Gospel that saved you.

Further, it must now be your profound goal to please Him in everything you do each and every day for the rest of your life. Certain verses are abundantly clear about these things. They are biblical truths that we must believe and embrace in order to obtain the confidence that we are truly children of God. By being sure of these things, we will have the assurance of spending eternity with our Creator, our King, and our personal Savior.

Please read the following verses over and over to fully grasp their significance:

"But he was wounded for our transgressions, he was bruised for our iniquities: the chastisement of our peace was upon him; and with his stripes we are healed. All we like sheep have gone astray; we have turned every one to his own way; and the LORD hath laid on him the iniquity of us all" (Isaiah 53:5–6).

"Who his own self bare our sins in his own body on the tree, that we, being dead to sins, should live unto righteousness: by whose stripes ye were healed" (1st Peter 2:24).

"But as many as received him, to them gave he power to become the sons of God, even to them that believe on his name: Which were born, not of blood, nor of the will of the flesh, nor of the will of man, but of God" (John 1:12–13).

"He that believeth on the Son hath everlasting life: and he that believeth not the Son shall not see life; but the wrath of God abideth on him" (John 3:36).

Chapter 4

On The Road To Damascus:
"What Shall I Do Lord?"

This living transmission, accomplished in the Holy Spirit, is called Tradition, since it is distinct from Sacred Scripture, though closely connected to it. Through Tradition, "the Church, in her doctrine, life, and worship perpetuates and transmits to every generation all that she herself is, all that she believes." "The sayings of the holy Fathers are a witness to the life-giving presence of this Tradition, showing how its riches are poured out in the practice and life of the Church, in her belief and her prayer.

The Catechism of the Catholic Church - 78

"And if any man shall take away from the words of the book of this prophecy, God shall take away his part out of the book of life, and out of the holy city, and from the things which are written in this book."

Revelation 22:19

Acts 5:34, reads in part, *"Then stood there up one in the council, a Pharisee, named Gamaliel, a doctor of the law, had in reputation among all the people..."*

One of Gamaliel's star pupils was a young, well-bred and rising Pharisee named Saul of Tarsus.

Not only was Saul dedicated to the persecution of Christians, he was also totally dedicated to preserving the teaching of the doctrines that the Pharisees had established. These doctrines were based on the tradition of men.

Jesus said, *"...Thus have ye made the commandment of God of none effect by your tradition"* (Matthew 15:6).

As a result of Saul's zealous defense of man's doctrine, he became a persecutor of the true doctrine believers embraced. He was as anti-Jesus as anyone could possibly be.

Subsequently, however, outside of Jesus Christ Himself, perhaps no one has had a more positive effect on the spread of the Gospel of Jesus Christ than Saul of Tarsus. Let's review the story of Saul in his own words from the book of Acts, chapter 22:

"I am verily a man which am a Jew, born in Tarsus, a city in Cilicia, yet brought up in this city at the feet of Gamaliel, and taught according to the perfect manner of the law of the fathers, and was zealous toward God, as ye all are this day. And I persecuted this way unto the death, binding and delivering into prisons both men and women. As also the high priest doth bear me witness, and all the estate of the elders: from whom also I received letters unto the brethren, and went to Damascus, to bring them which were there bound unto Jerusalem, for to be punished. And it came to pass, that, as I made my journey, and was come nigh unto Damascus about noon, suddenly there shone from heaven a great light round about me. And I fell unto the

ground, and heard a voice saying unto me, Saul, Saul, why persecutest thou me? And I answered, Who art thou, Lord? And he said unto me, I am Jesus of Nazareth, whom thou persecutest. And they that were with me saw indeed the light, and were afraid; but they heard not the voice of him that spake to me. And I said, What shall I do, Lord? And the Lord said unto me, Arise, and go into Damascus; and there it shall be told thee of all things which are appointed for thee to do. And when I could not see for the glory of that light, being led by the hand of them that were with me, I came into Damascus. And one Ananias, a devout man according to the law, having a good report of all the Jews which dwelt there, Came unto me, and stood, and said unto me, Brother Saul, receive thy sight. And the same hour I looked up upon him. And he said, The God of our fathers hath chosen thee, that thou shouldest know his will, and see that Just One, and shouldest hear the voice of his mouth. For thou shalt be his witness unto all men of what thou hast seen and heard. And now why tarriest thou? arise, and be baptized, and wash away thy sins, calling on the name of the Lord. And it came to pass, that, when I was come again to Jerusalem, even while I prayed in the temple, I was in a trance; And saw him saying unto me, Make haste, and get thee quickly out of Jerusalem: for they will not receive thy testimony concerning me. And I said, Lord, they know that I imprisoned and beat in every synagogue them that believed on thee: And when the blood of thy martyr Stephen was shed, I also was standing by, and consenting unto his death, and kept the raiment of them that slew him. And he said unto me, Depart: for I will send thee far hence unto the Gentiles. And they gave him audience unto this word, and then lifted up their voices, and said, Away with such a fellow from the earth: for it is not fit that he should live. And as they cried out, and cast off their clothes, and threw dust into the air, The chief captain commanded him to be brought into the castle, and bade that he should be examined by scourging; that he might know wherefore they cried so against him. And as they bound him with thongs, Paul said unto the centurion that stood by, Is it lawful for you to scourge a man that is a Roman, and uncondemned? When the centurion heard that, he went and told the chief captain, saying, Take heed what thou doest: for this man is a Roman. Then the chief captain came, and said unto him, Tell me, art thou a Roman? He said, Yea. And the chief captain answered, With a great sum obtained I this freedom. And Paul said, But I was free born. Then straightway they departed from him which should have examined him: and the chief captain also was afraid, after he knew that he was a Roman, and because he had bound him. On the morrow, because he would have known the certainty wherefore he was accused of the Jews, he loosed him from his bands, and commanded the chief priests and all their council to appear, and brought Paul down, and set him before them" (Acts 22:3–31).

What an exciting testimony of the conversion of a man who vehemently defended tradition but who met the Word of God in person!

Catholic readers, please note that it was Jesus Christ Himself who sent Saul of Tarsus, who later became the apostle Paul, to minister to the Gentiles. Had God wanted to create the office of pope, He probably would have seen to it that Paul, not Peter, would have been installed.

In my opinion, Paul turned out to be the greatest of the apostles. He wrote thirteen books of the New Testament: Romans, 1st and 2nd Corinthians, Galatians, Ephesians,

Philippians, Colossians, 1st and 2nd Thessalonians, 1st and 2nd Timothy, Titus and Philemon.

Most scholars believe that Paul also wrote the book of Hebrews. Peter wrote just two books, 1st and 2nd Peter, both of which are relatively short in length. But most important of all, at least to this writer, is the meaning in the message of Saul's (Paul's) journey on the road to Damascus. In this journey, I find a very important parallel to my own life, and I truly hope and pray that you will also have "a road to Damascus" experience that causes similar life-changing results.

As indicated at the outset of this book, I practiced Catholicism for 64 years. A zealot for the faith, I had the benefit of the best available Catholic grammar and high schools.

Like Saul, who passed along the teachings of Gamaliel, I passed along with great enthusiasm what I learned to anyone who would listen.

However, the Lord started to transform me from the knowledge of untruth to the knowledge of truth. He didn't choose to knock me to the ground blinded, but He worked on me persistently. I sent away for tapes and books, and subscribed to the publications of competent Bible scholars and teachers. Everything I received was predicated on the inerrancy of the Word of God.

Above all, I increased my Bible reading on a daily basis. It didn't take me very long to realize that most of Catholicism is almost totally grounded on the precepts of men. Yes, there is a belief in Jesus Christ, but the Church of Rome has added an endless list of allegedly "infallible" doctrines and dogma which are unbiblical. Portions of this Tradition emanating from the minds of men have been rescinded and sometimes even reinstated over the years, proof in itself that neither the doctrine, nor the sponsoring church can claim infallibility. That is a common sense assessment. A committee of theologians is not required to figure it out or rule on it; it's a no-brainer!

The Vatican has made many declarations that Jesus Christ's redemptive work at Calvary is not sufficient for salvation. Mostly all of the church councils, such as Trent and Vatican II officially attest to this.

And again, as mentioned earlier, many popes throughout history have sponsored atrocities against Christians who believe in an inerrant Bible. The Inquisitions are just one example on a list of many.

This gives proof of the testimony of a young firebrand priest that my fianceé and I listened to at "pre-cana" (pre-wedding) conferences we attended in 1955. The priest said, "The way we know that the Catholic Church is the one true church is that it survived the most vile and diabolical history imaginable."

If you decide to study church history, you will be appalled by your findings. Mike Gendron, a devout Catholic for 37 years, experienced a "road to Damascus" conversion himself and went on to become a graduate of Dallas Theological Seminary. He summarizes the subject well:

"By the 12th century, the Roman Catholic Church had become the world's most powerful institution. It used its unlimited religious and political power to set up and depose kings and queens. It taxed people mercilessly and confiscated property to become the richest institution on Earth. Popes offered crusading armies riches and eternal bliss to kill Muslims, heretics, and anyone who rejected papal supremacy. *'For all nations have drunk of the wine of the wrath of her fornication, and the kings of the Earth have committed fornication with her, and the merchants of the Earth are waxed rich through the abundance of her delica-*

cies' (Revelation 18:3). After the Reformation in the 16th century, the Catholic Church lost its status as the official state church in most parts of the world and could no longer put her opponents to death. The strategy is to unite all the religions of the world through common moral values." [1]

The Catholic Church of today has become very caught up in the Ecumenical Movement which, of course, Mike Gendron refers to.

The Bible clearly states that during the endtimes there will be a one-world religion. It's coming on strong and the Bible connects the universal church with the Antichrist, the one-world government, one-world currency and one-world economy. Oh, yes, the coming one-world religion is even associated with the number 666! Fasten your seat belts; it's going to get very interesting!

[1] Mike Gendron, *Roman Catholicism – Scripture vs. Tradition* (tract), Proclaiming The Gospel, P.O. Box 940871, Plano, TX 75094.

Chapter 5

Pope John Paul II Claims He Will Control The New World Order

'We teach and define that it is a dogma divinely revealed: that the Roman Pontiff, when he speaks *ex cathedra*, that is, when in discharge of the office of pastor and doctor of all Christians, by virtue of his supreme Apostolic authority, he defines a doctrine regarding faith and morals to be held by the universal Church, by the divine assistance promised him in blessed Peter, is possessed of that infallibility with which the divine Redeemer willed that his Church should be endowed for defining doctrine regarding faith or morals; and that therefore such definitions of the Roman Pontiff are irreformable of themselves, and not from the consent of the Church. But if any one—which may God avert—presume to contradict this our definition: let him be anathema.

Vatican One—Dogmatic Decrees of the Vatican Council
Concerning the Infallible Teaching of the Roman Pontiff, Chapter IV

*"And they continued stedfastly in the apostles' **doctrine** and fellowship, and in breaking of bread, and in prayers."*

Acts 2:42

The Bible clearly indicates that in the last days there will be only one global government, economy, and religion. These circumstances are approaching with lightning speed!

For example, former president George Bush used the term "A New World Order" over 200 times in his speeches.

It seems that we have all been preconditioned for the year 2000, and the implications that the turn of the millennium will thrust us into the "New Age." Eventually, we will be on our way to becoming constituents of a new international government, a "New World Order."

Where individual countries have previously been independent of each other, Europe has shown an inexorable movement toward unification.

In fact, Europeans have already adopted a single currency known as the euro, and are functioning within a borderless society. These developments, which would have been considered impossible just 10 to 20 years ago, have been paving the way for the European Union to provide the governmental nucleus for the advent of a world-wide dictator.

The Bible also declares that just prior to these last-days events, the Body of Christ, those who have trusted exclusively in Jesus Christ for their salvation, will be taken from the earth. Christians refer to this event as the Rapture of the Church.

Following this translation of believers from earth to heaven, the man destined to become the unchallenged global leader will emerge on the world scene. The remaining world population will be introduced to the biblically-heralded Antichrist.

According to Malachi Martin's book, *The Keys Of This Blood*, when the Antichrist emerges, the reigning pope will aggressively seek control. This attempt to grab power may include more than just the desire to control the world-wide religious system.

Even the pope expresses a similar New World Order view in Martin's book, which details "the grand design's" intricacies. According to Martin, the pope claims that he will lead this New World Order government system by the year 2000. The subtitle on the book's cover says it all: "...Pope John Paul II Versus Russia And The West For Control Of The New World Order." [1]

Malachi Martin is a foremost apologist for the Catholic faith and is largely acknowledged as a close friend of Pope John Paul II.

Even though the new Catholic Catechism proclaims Holy Scripture as the inspired Word of God, many within and outside the Church of Rome proclaim otherwise. Nevertheless, as we continue to race toward the New World Order, it will become evident, even to skeptics, that the Bible is totally accurate in describing these events.

How can one not be impressed that prophecies unfolding before our eyes today were written over 2500 years ago in the book of Daniel and almost 2000 years ago in the book of Revelation?

True believers, members of the Body of Christ, won't be around when the Antichrist takes total control of the lives of every human being left on earth. Those who are not taken with His Church will find it impossible to escape the awful and relentless torments described in the Bible, those events that will take place during the last three and a half years of the tribulation period.

The first half of that time period will be marked by peace, prosperity, and economic success, but the second half will be hell on earth. Read Matthew 24:21–22: *"For then shall be great tribulation, such as was not since the beginning of the world to this time, no, nor ever shall be. And except those days should be short-*

ened, there should no flesh be saved: but for the elect's sake those days shall be shortened."

Mark 13:19–20 reads, *"For in those days shall be affliction, such as was not from the beginning of the creation which God created unto this time, neither shall be. And except that the Lord had shortened those days, no flesh should be saved: but for the elect's sake, whom he hath chosen, he hath shortened the days."*

God Himself will intervene during these events:

"And except those days should be shortened, there should no flesh be saved..." (Matthew 24:22).

When was the last time you heard about the tribulation from a Catholic pulpit? Although the Vatican declares the Bible to be the inspired Word of God, it acts is if God is only right in just some Scripture. The Vatican, comprised of mere men, seems to feel it must correct things by not disclosing all of His Word to their congregations. Or, equally reprehensible, the Church of Rome adds its own ideas and then labels them infallible.

Discerning the truth about such matters encompasses eternal consequences for the reader. The Vatican is very much opposed to your doing this.

An article from the March 1994 edition of *The State* newspaper speaks about the "130–page document" the Vatican had written to counter non-Catholic interpretations of the Bible.[2]

A new Vatican document on how to interpret the Bible condemns the fundamentalist approach as distorting and possibly leading to racism. The 130–page document...is the Roman Catholic Church's latest commentary on trends in Biblical study. Some of its language is unusually harsh, reflecting the challenge that fundamentalists pose to the church.

"Without saying as much, in so many words, fundamen-

talism actually invites people to intellectual suicide," says
the document from the Pontifical Biblical Commission. The
authors save their harshest language for Christian fundamentalist denominations, which have been posing a challenge to
the Roman church, particularly in Latin America... "The
fundamentalist approach is dangerous, for it is attractive to
people who look to the Bible for ready answers to the problems of life."

— *The State*, March 19, 1994, p.D8

Commenting on the above article entitled, "Pontifical
Biblical Commission," author Arno Froese relates that:

"The brutal and oppressive language the Vatican uses in this
report reveals her great fear of losing her stranglehold on
hundreds of millions led astray by her false doctrines such as
the pope's infallibility, purgatory, the Eucharist, the rosary,
the worship of the dead, worship of Mary, plus other cultic
religious activities that are contrary to the precious Word of
God.

"Vatican doctrine, at the zenith of its visible wickedness,
led to the sale of 'indulgences,' that is, the forgiveness of
sins through the payment of money to the Roman treasury.

"Yes, indeed, the fundamentalist (Bible) approach is dangerous to the Vatican, because it can liberate lost souls from
the bondage of a man-made religion and lead them to the lib-
erty in Jesus Christ through the preaching of the Gospel." [2]

And so, rarely, if ever, will anyone hear Catholic pulpit
readings from the books of Daniel, Revelation, or other
prophetic books such as Ezekiel, Isaiah, Ruth and Jeremiah.
These books contain the unchanging truth of God's
Word. Over the years the Vatican has adulterated His Word
which is an abomination to the Lord.

This is one reason why some Bible scholars identify the reference in Revelation 17:5 *"MYSTERY, BABYLON THE GREAT, THE MOTHER OF HARLOTS AND ABOMINATIONS OF THE EARTH"* as the last-days world-wide religion led by the Church of Rome.

[1]Malachi Martin, *The Keys Of This Blood*, Doubleday, as reported in *U.S. News and World Report*, June 10, 1996.

[2]Arno Froese, *How Democracy Will Elect the Antichrist*, The Olive Press, Columbia, SC, 1997. p.103–104.

Chapter 6

The Great Tribulation:
Three and A Half Years Of Peace and Prosperity, Three and A Half Years Of Hell On Earth

Before Christ's second coming the Church must pass through a final trial that will shake the faith of many believers. The persecution that accompanies her pilgrimage on earth will unveil the "mystery of iniquity" in the form of a religious deception offering men an apparent solution to their problems at the price of apostasy from the truth. The supreme religious deception is that of the Antichrist, a pseudo-messianism by which man glorifies himself in place of God and of his Messiah come in the flesh.

The Catechism of the Catholic Church - 675

"For then shall be great tribulation, such as was not since the beginning of the world to this time, no, nor ever shall be. And except those days should be shortened, there should no flesh be saved: but for the elect's sake those days shall be shortened."

Matthew 24:21-22

"And he causeth all, both small and great, rich and poor, free and bond, to receive a mark in their right hand, or in their foreheads: And that no man might buy or sell, save he that had the mark, or the name of the beast, or the number of his name. Here is wisdom. Let him that hath understanding count the number of the beast: for it is the number of a man; and his number is Six hundred threescore and six" (Revelation 13:16–18).

John wrote the above passage almost 2,000 years ago. Can you imagine writing a prophecy like that in an environment with no technical knowledge or equipment of even the crudest kind?

Today, the technology exists to do exactly what John predicted. Author Terry Cook has devoted much of his energy to documenting that the technology described in John's prediction is available right now!

Only a reluctant public is holding back the government's attempt to implement what could be called the "666 system." I have read Terry Cook's book, *The Mark of the New World Order*, and also studied other video tapes on the subject. The following is a synopsis of these materials.

Each one of us can be fitted with a radio frequency biochip transponder the size of a grain of rice or smaller. This can be painlessly injected under the skin, probably in our hand. This device is capable of holding 2000 pages of information. Think of this as being part of the same technology as the bar code system used at supermarket checkouts.

If everyone was forced to utilize this system, the scenario as prophesied by the Apostle John could be made operational now! One of the reasons that the first three and a half years of the Tribulation Period—the time marked by peace—works so well is that virtually everyone left on the planet is thrust into a cashless society. This economic structure will eliminate such problems as the underground economy, tax fraud, money laundering and illegal drug transactions. All of these problems cost taxpayers lots of money. But not when everyone is forced to submit to the scanner, which will rule out all 'lawbreakers.'

What about convenience? How many times have you been in the checkout line at the supermarket, behind someone fussing with a credit-card or writing a check for a $2 order? No longer a problem! Members of the cashless society will simply put their hands on the scanner (assuming that is where their transponder has been placed). The amount will be deducted from the purchaser's account and credited to the food retailer's account. People may never even have to go to the bank. Everything will be electronically entered and received via home computer. Think of all the government bureaucracies, including the IRS, that will be eliminated or at least drastically reduced as a result of these developments. Everyone, it seems will be as happy as clams. Yes, those first three and a half years will be just glorious!

Then an earth-shattering event will take place. The world leader, the Antichrist, who will have gained unchallenged total international power, will institute a binding dictum on all. People won't be able to buy or sell unless they have received his mark, thereby declaring allegiance to him, an allegiance so strong that they also will have to declare him as God. Taking the mark will result in eternal condemnation since one could never escape the allegiance in order to accept Christ.

The Antichrist will triumphantly enter the newly built Jewish Temple in Jerusalem, declaring himself as God. Devastation will befall all mankind. Some scholars believe that there will be full-scale nuclear exchanges among major powers and even among other smaller countries.[1]

The wrath of the true God will have commenced. We don't want to be around when all this takes place. Other parts of this book detail how the Word of God instructs you on how to escape this fate. Even if you are not alive during the tribulation period, the same procedure will assure you of your personal salvation now. Read on!

Why does God condemn those receiving the mark of the beast? Because doing so indicates that person has accepted the Antichrist as their God. Prior to the tribulation period, God wanted that person to accept His Son as the exclusive means of escaping the tribulation and attaining eternal security. That's why God raptures His Son's true Church prior to the tribulation period. That explains why Jesus, through the apostle John, said:

"I am come in my Father's name, and ye receive me not: if another shall come in his own name, him ye will receive." (John 5:43).

[1]Terry L. Cook, *The Mark of the New World Order*, Virtue International Publishing.

Chapter 7

You, the Rapture
and Decision Time

The Church encourages us to prepare ourselves for the hour of our death. In the litany of the saints, for instance, she has us pray: "From a sudden and unforeseen death, deliver us, O Lord"; to ask the Mother of God to interceded for us "at the hour of our death" in the *Hail Mary*; and to entrust ourselves to St. Joseph, the patron saint of a happy death.

The Catechism of the Catholic Church - 1014

"In whom ye also trusted, after that ye heard the word of truth, the gospel of your salvation: in whom also after that ye believed, ye were sealed with that holy Spirit of promise, Which is the earnest of our inheritance until the redemption of the purchased possession, unto the praise of his glory."

Ephesians 1:13-14

Earlier in this book, I listed 18 expositors of the Word of God whose work I study consistently. I cannot help but notice that they are increasingly and excitingly underscoring the biblical truth. They firmly believe that the Lord of their heart, Jesus Christ, will be coming soon to snatch His Church from earth and take her with Him to heaven!

That may be big news for Catholics, but unfortunately it is a rare message in many Protestant congregations these days. Nevertheless, the Bible clearly states that Jesus Christ will come for His Church "in the clouds." Scripture also states that no one knows the exact time this will occur:

"But of that day and that hour knoweth no man, no, not the angels which are in heaven, neither the Son, but the Father" (Mark 13:32).

However, we are instructed to be on the lookout for the biblical signs of His coming. Those 18 scholars and others are united in their belief that when Israel became a nation in 1948, the count-down pointing to our Lord's coming for His Church began.

Other signs of the immanency of Christ's return include difficult-to-treat diseases such as AIDS and other plagues, increasingly violent and/or otherwise unusual weather, declining standards of morality, an exponential increase in general knowledge, and rapid progress toward a unified world government and religion, as well as the *"wars and rumors of wars"* mentioned in Matthew 24:6.

But perhaps the most abominable endtime sign is the continual compromise of God's Word. The Bible warns of great deception during the last days, satanic deception that manifests itself not only from outside the Church, but from within as well!

"For there shall arise false Christs, and false prophets, and shall shew great signs and wonders; insomuch that, if it were possible, they shall deceive the very elect" (Matthew 24:24).

Although apostasy has been a problem since the earliest days of the Church, we are seeing more and more evidence of it today even within the professing evangelical community.

Although Catholics do not hear much about the coming of Jesus Christ for His Church, they may hear messages about the Second Coming. But it is important to point out that these are *two separate events*. Christ will first come *for* His Church and then He will come again (Second Coming) *with* His Church.

While the word "Rapture" does not appear in the Bible, it is described in 1st Corinthians and 1st Thessalonians. The latter says it all:

"For the Lord himself shall descend from heaven with a shout, with the voice of the archangel, and with the trump of God: and the dead in Christ shall rise first: Then we which are alive and remain shall be caught up together with them in the clouds, to meet the Lord in the air: and so shall we ever be with the Lord" (1st Thessalonians 4:16–17).

Sadly, the Catholic Church cannot teach this wonderful and encouraging biblical truth because it conflicts with the Vatican's own humanly-conceived writings labeled as infallible.

Common sense must have alerted you by now that the two sides of this issue cannot both be correct. How can the *Catechism of the Catholic Church* teach that the Bible is the inspired work of the Holy Spirit, and then fail to teach its flock some of the most important aspects of that work?

You will have to make a decision. You must either accept the inspired Word of God or the precepts of men. They cannot co-exist.

Reflect on this passage of Scripture and then read 1st Corinthians 15:51–53, *"Behold, I shew you a mystery; We shall not all sleep, but we shall all be changed, In a moment, in the twinkling of an eye, at the last trump: for the trumpet shall sound, and the dead shall be raised incorruptible, and we shall be changed. For this corruptible must put on incorruption, and this mortal must put on immortality."*

The Holy Spirit is trying to get your attention! Don't resist Him! And remember this: The Catechism says nothing about His Church, the Body of Christ, accompanying the Lord during the Second Coming.

The Body of Christ will rule with Jesus over the earth during the Millennium. Are you a member of the Body of Christ? Will you be among that congregation? Most Catholics will not! They have been deceived by a false gospel which promises salvation through the sacraments, transubstantiation, attendance at Mass, purgatory, indulgences and other extra-biblical doctrines.

Decision time is now! Does your heart truly call out to accept the Word of God rather than the precepts of men? If so, please recite this prayer with every ounce of sincerity and conviction that you can muster:

Dear Heavenly Father, I repent of all my sins: past, present, and future. I firmly believe that your Holy Spirit has convicted me to obey your will by accepting your Son's shed blood on my behalf as the exclusive means for my salvation. I accept this unmerited gift of grace through faith. I believe Jesus died in obedience to the Father and because of His love for me.

I now accept Jesus Christ into my heart and mind as

personal Savior and Lord of my life! Based on His Word, I believe He now lives in me through the presence of the Holy Spirit.

I now commit my life to doing Your will as found only in Your Word, the Holy Bible.

In Jesus' name, I offer this prayer, Amen.

If you petitioned God the Father with those or very similar words, from a truly contrite and sincere heart, you have become a member of the Body of Christ. You will experience the Rapture and shall always be with the Lord!

Chapter 8

The Alternative:
The Wages of Sin

Venial sin allows charity to subsist, even though it offends and wounds it.

Mortal sin, by attacking the vital principle within us - that is, charity - necessitates a new initiative of God's mercy and a conversion of heart which is normally accomplished within the setting of the sacrament of reconciliation.

The Catechism of the Catholic Church - 1855, 1856

"For the wages of sin is death; but the gift of God is eternal life through Jesus Christ our Lord."

Romans 6:23

At this point, some Catholic readers will have made a decision affecting their eternity. They will have sincerely, therefore successfully, petitioned God through His Son to save them from their sins.

Others will say, "It just can't be possible; it seems all too simple." During your life, the church has instructed that you need to perform an endless amount of works to be saved. Through this teaching, the Catholic Church has placed you, and one billion other followers under needless bondage. In direct opposition, the apostle Paul sums up the Bible's message very simply and concisely in just 21 words: *"For the wages of sin is death; but the gift of God is eternal life through Jesus Christ our Lord"* (Romans 6:23).

Nothing in the Word of God even remotely suggests that subsequent to its complete writings, *"...all the counsel of God,"* (Acts 20:27) that there would be a need for additional human counsel.

The Church of Rome has allowed its addendum, Catholic Tradition, to progress in importance to the point at which it now outweighs the importance of Scripture.

Nor does Scripture mention the need for a religious institution to be established in order to decipher the Word of God. However, the Vatican has established such a body: the Magisterium. Page 29 of the Catechism (#95) says:

> "...God, sacred Tradition, Sacred Scripture, and the
> Magisterium of the Church are so connected and associated
> that one of them cannot stand without the others."

This is a remarkable statement, especially in light of the fact that the Catechism indicates that Holy Scripture is the inerrant Word of God. The inerrant Word of God doesn't contain a single verse even remotely suggesting the need for sacred tradition or a Magisterium.

If you decide to talk to your parish priest about this matter, you may find he has difficulty in explaining these contradictions because all he can tell you is based on the Catholic Tradition, which is not scriptural. The Bible and Catechism are in hopeless conflict.

The Bible teaches that God detests the traditions of men, and implores us to read our own Bible daily.

"Howbeit in vain do they worship me, teaching for doctrines the commandments of men. For laying aside the commandment of God, ye hold the tradition of men, as the washing of pots and cups: and many other such like things ye do" (Mark 7:7–8).

"These were more noble than those in Thessalonica, in that they received the word with all readiness of mind, and searched the scriptures daily, whether those things were so" (Acts 17:11).

As for an excellent summary of what God foreknew would happen, read the following:

"For the time will come when they will not endure sound doctrine; but after their own lusts shall they heap to themselves teachers, having itching ears; And they shall turn away their ears from the truth, and shall be turned unto fables" (2nd Timothy 4:3–4).

Until anyone exclusively accepts biblical truth, he or she will be living in the domain of darkness:

"Who hath delivered us from the power of darkness, and hath translated us into the kingdom of his dear Son: In whom we have redemption through his blood, even the forgiveness of sins" (Colossians 1:13–14).

During my last ten years of faithful Sunday Mass attendance I witnessed a significant increase in philosophically-toned messages from the pulpit.

Although three passages of Scripture were usually read, a philosophical message always seemed to be the goal for each homily. Often the homily didn't include an exposition of the Scripture at all.

If you have made a decision for Christ and you are now a born again Christian, don't be deceived by such philosophical messages any longer, no matter how persuasive they may seem. Hold on to, and be guided by the precious truth, the pure Word of God. Focus on your personal Savior and Lord, Jesus Christ.

"Beware lest any man spoil you through philosophy and vain deceit, after the tradition of men, after the rudiments of the world, and not after Christ" (Colossians 2:8).

The apostle Paul knew that those who exclusively believe in the Word would be challenged by unbelievers with humanly-conceived doctrines. He advised His beloved friend Timothy:

"O Timothy, keep that which is committed to thy trust, avoiding profane and vain babblings, and oppositions of science falsely so called: Which some professing have erred concerning the faith. Grace be with thee. Amen" (1st Timothy 6:20–21).

Chapter 9

Your Moment of Truth

The Church affirms that for believers the sacraments of the New Covenant are *necessary for salvation*. "Sacramental grace" is the grace of the Holy Spirit, given by Christ and proper to each sacrament. The Spirit heals and transforms those who receive him by conforming them to the Son of God. The fruit of the sacramental life is that the Spirit of adoption makes the faithful partakers in the divine nature by uniting them in a living union with the only Son, the Savior.

The Catechism of the Catholic Church - 1129
The Council of Trent

"And brought them out, and said, Sirs, what must I do to be saved? And they said, Believe on the Lord Jesus Christ, and thou shalt be saved, and thy house."

Acts 16:30-31

We must now address the pragmatic and provocative title of this book, *When Catholics Die*, and its inference, "What happens?"

The Son of God, Jesus Christ, provides the following answer:

"...Verily, verily, I say unto thee, Except a man be born again, he cannot see the kingdom of God" (John 3:3).

If you are a new born again Christian, I sincerely recommend that you join a Bible-believing congregation or Bible study group. Don't wait; do it now! But I must add a caveat: Many who leave Catholicism to join such congregations receive ridicule from family and friends. I know from personal experience just how discomforting this can be.

Some people to who I have been closest have labeled me as some sort of "fire and brimstone" preacher. This is so sad because if they took the time to carefully study the Catholic Catechism and the Bible they would become troubled. They would realize that Catholic Tradition and virtually all other Catholic doctrines are anti-scriptural.

Yes, there is some pain in conversion, but most of us turn away from the hurt because we know that we must now concentrate on our Savior's will for our lives and no longer be sensitive to the ridicule of men.

Chapter 10

Be Good and Go To Hell

The divine image is present in every man. It shines forth in the communion of persons, in the likeness of the union of the divine persons among themselves.

The Catechism of the Catholic Church - 1702

"But we are all as an unclean thing, and all our right-eousnesses are as filthy rags; and we all do fade as a leaf; and our iniquities, like the wind, have taken us away. And there is none that calleth upon thy name, that stirreth up himself to take hold of thee: for thou hast hid thy face from us, and hast consumed us, because of our iniquities."

Isaiah 64:6-7

According to Scripture, striving to be righteous in the eyes of God is commendable although meaningless unless we've been born again by the Spirit of God. If we have not been born again, all of our righteousness is for naught — we're not hitting any "home runs" in the eyes of God. He hides His face from those who believe that they can earn salvation by the righteousness of doing good works.

"But we are all as an unclean thing, and all our righteousnesses are as filthy rags; and we all do fade as a leaf; and our iniquities, like the wind, have taken us away. And there is none that calleth upon thy name, that stirreth up himself to take hold of thee: for thou hast hid thy face from us, and hast consumed us, because of our iniquities" (Isaiah 64:6–7).

Initially it was very difficult for me to accept verses such as these. For over 50 years, I had been taught that a myriad of works, in addition to Jesus Christ, was necessary to earn salvation. But, God's Word overwhelmingly says we must rely on Christ's atoning death at Calvary as the exclusive means for salvation. Nothing else matters insofar as the remission of all sins is concerned. Only after a person is born again do works become important.

Whenever I've tried to witness the truth to Catholics, I've been shunned by attitudes like these:

"How can you be right and the Catholic Church be wrong?"

"They're big and powerful, so they must be right and you must be wrong!"

"How can you know more than they do?"

"How can the pope's teachings be wrong? He is God's representative on earth."

Those responses please the Vatican. But dear reader, it is not what the Word of God wants you to believe.

The Holy Scripture teaches that those who resist the Word of God will become blinded to the truth. Think long and hard. Has this happened to you? Have you allowed non-scriptural teachings to blind you from the truth? Please read and re-read the following Scriptures and see if the Word of God, through the inspiration of the Holy Spirit, is describing you in this passage.

"But if our gospel be hid, it is hid to them that are lost: In whom the god of this world hath blinded the minds of them which believe not, lest the light of the glorious gospel of Christ, who is the image of God, should shine unto them" (2nd Corinthians 4:3–4).

There is just one mediator between God and man. There is absolutely no scriptural evidence for the need of a pope, the Vatican, or a Magisterium to intercede between God and man. Nor is there one shred of evidence even suggesting that man-made doctrines and dogmas of Scripture — Catholic Tradition — are necessary for our salvation.

"For there is one God, and one mediator between God and men, the man Christ Jesus" (1st Timothy 2:5).

"My little children, these things write I unto you, that ye sin not. And if any man sin, we have an advocate with the Father, Jesus Christ the righteous: And he is the propitiation for our sins: and not for ours only, but also for the sins of the whole world" (1st John 2:1–2).

"Add thou not unto his words, lest he reprove thee, and thou be found a liar" (Proverbs 30:6).

As we already discussed, God views a lost person's attempt to use good works in order to please Him as an attempt at self-righteousness that is nothing better than filthy rags. Here is another Scripture passage that describes our offering of filthy rags in much more descriptive language:

"Now Joshua was clothed with filthy garments, and stood before the angel. And he answered and spake unto those that stood before him, saying, Take away the filthy garments from him. And unto him he said, Behold, I have caused thine iniquity to pass from thee, and I will clothe thee with change of raiment" (Zechariah 3:3–4).

Chuck Missler, a leading expositor of the Word, points out that the Hebrew root word translated as "filthy" means "excrement-bespattered."[1]

Let's try to paint a picture of what was taking place. Joshua was the high priest of the Jewish people, the highest rank attainable. We might compare him to the pope, but unfortunately this is a faulty analogy because, as we have already illustrated, Scripture doesn't even suggest that believers require a human high priest of any kind.

The Lord takes away Joshua's sins and replaces his excrement-bespattered garments. Think of it this way: Only God can remove even the pope's sins. No system of Catholic theology, doctrines, dogmas, decrees or other forms of restorative works can do it. Only the exclusive belief in Jesus Christ can take away our sins because Jesus Christ is our High Priest. Scripture confirms this for God's elect:

"Who shall lay any thing to the charge of God's elect? It is God that justifieth. Who is he that condemneth? It is Christ that died, yea rather, that is risen again, who is even at the right hand of God, who also maketh intercession for us" (Romans 8:33–34).

The Christian Church survived the first fifteen centuries before Tradition became equal to God's Word in importance.

At the Council of Trent in 1545 Catholic Tradition was declared equal in authority with the Bible. That's certainly remarkable when you think of the enormity of this. Mere men declared that their word is equal in authority to God's Word! How vain and deceitful these men were and continue to be to this very day! God knows the past, present and future simultaneously. That is why, through the apostle Paul, He declared: *"Beware lest any man spoil you through philosophy and vain deceit, after the tradition of men, after the rudiments of the world, and not after Christ"* (Colossians 2:8).

The battle for the minds of men, women and children, by the opposing viewpoints of born again Christians and the Vatican, goes on and on.

You may be surprised that this author believes this battle, prior to the Rapture, will eventually be won by the apostate Church of Rome. But it's really not a difficult conclusion to reach for anyone who studies the Bible because the Word teaches that there will be just one world-wide religion during the endtimes.

Anyone with even a rudimentary understanding of current events will detect an inexorable Ecumenical Movement and the Vatican's leadership toward establishing one universal church. And so it will be: The tradition of men will appear to overcome the Word of God.

The Lord of heaven and earth will condemn those who have promulgated this deceit. He has been cursing all false teachers to eternal damnation ever since the death of His beloved Son, Jesus Christ. The apostle Paul forewarned the perpetrators about this judgment, and then warned them again in the very next passage of Scripture:

"But though we, or an angel from heaven, preach any other gospel unto you than that which we have preached unto you, let him be accursed. As we said before, so say I now again, if any man preach any other gospel unto you than that ye have received, let him be accursed" (Galatians 1:8–9).

That's a very powerful warning! False teachers, like anyone else, can come to Christ and be saved. Let us all pray to the Savior that they do!

The Bible clearly teaches why man-made doctrines, in this case Catholic Tradition, oppose the will of God. In His omniscience, knew that these false doctrines would be instituted. That's why His Word clearly states His will regarding these things. Have you looked for these truths in your Bible, or do you continue to be deceived by non-biblical Catholic Tradition? Your eternity is at stake!

"Not by works of righteousness which we have done, but according to his mercy he saved us..." (Titus 3:5).

How has the Catholic Church condemned born again Christians who have exclusively followed God's Word rather than the precepts of men? How have they condemned those who do not believe all the doctrines and dogmas of the Catholic Church? Both groups have been cursed with numerous anathemas.[2]

Church councils have "infallibly" declared that anyone who doesn't believe in even one of the Catholic doctrines has been turned over to God for condemnation! Every Catholic should think about this long and hard. If you don't believe in just one doctrine — purgatory, for example — your church has condemned you!

You also are cursed with an anathema if you believe the short Bible verse above, or the many other Bible verses that essentially say the same thing—that you have been saved by the grace of God and are justified by faith alone.

The Councils of Trent and Vatican II have instituted over 100 anathemas to all those who have refused to believe even one Catholic doctrine or who believe exclusively in Jesus Christ for their salvation. Your conclusion should be: "With respect to my eternal salvation, it's dangerous having faith in Catholicism."

[1]Chuck Missler, *Expository Commentary: Zechariah,* Koinonia House, Cour'D'Alene, Idaho. 1997, p.45.

[2]Dave Hunt, *A Woman Rides The Beast,* Harvest House Publishers, 1994, p. 89-90.

Chapter 11

Saved by Works or Faith?

If anyone says that after the reception of the grace of justification the guilt is so remitted and the debt of eternal punishment so blotted out to every repentant sinner, that no debt of temporal punishment remains to be discharged either in this world or in purgatory before the gates of heaven can be opened, let him be anathema.

Council of Trent - Canon 30

"Much more then, being now justified by his blood, we shall be saved from wrath through him. For if, when we were enemies, we were reconciled to God by the death of his Son, much more, being reconciled, we shall be saved by his life."

Romans 5:9-10

The Church of Rome turns to the book of James to prove that works are necessary for salvation. Catholic apologists like to quote the following three verses without looking further into Scripture for any confirmation. These passages do indeed seem to make a strong case for works.

"What doth it profit, my brethren, though a man say he hath faith, and have not works? can faith save him?" (James 2:14).

"Even so faith, if it hath not works, is dead, being alone" (James 2:17).

"But wilt thou know, O vain man, that faith without works is dead?" (James 2:20).

Yes! By all means, our Savior wants to see good works and good deeds from His children, but not as their way to obtain salvation.

In the midst of those closely positioned verses in the book of James is a passage which provides a major clue as to how the born again Christian reconciles any discrepancies he senses regarding the "faith vs. works" issue:

"Yea, a man may say, Thou hast faith, and I have works; shew me thy faith without thy works, and I will shew thee my faith by my works'" (James 2:18).

Certain portions of the Bible apply only to those who are part of the Body of Christ. These passages are examples of this biblical truth. All four verses relate only to those who have been born again by the Spirit of God. To the lost, these verses simply have no meaning.

The first three tell the believer that true faith is verified by the good works expected by his Savior. God expects the believer, although assured of eternal security, to exhibit to everyone that he is a child of God. This is expressed well in the fourth passage. The example of works and faith is demonstrated in Abraham, as James 2:21–23 states,

"Was not Abraham our father justified by works, when he had offered Isaac his son upon the altar? Seest thou how faith wrought with his works, and by works was faith made perfect? And the scripture was fulfilled which saith, Abraham believed God, and it was imputed unto him for righteousness: and he was called the Friend of God."

Abraham was justified by works — works of faith. Abraham believed in the living God and that *"...was imputed unto him for righteousness...."* Even the harlot Rahab, who believed in the God of Israel and acted on that belief, was justified by works based on faith. Although we are justified by faith, we manifest this faith through our works. We can find a summation of this principle in the books of Galatians and Titus.

"Knowing that a man is not justified by the works of the law, but by the faith in Jesus Christ, even we have believed in Jesus Christ, that we might be justified by the faith in Christ, and not by the works of the law; for by the works of the law shall no flesh be justified" (Galatians 2:16).

"Not by works of righteousness which we have done, but according to his mercy he saved us, by the washing of regeneration, and renewing of the Holy Ghost; Which he shed on us abundantly through Jesus Christ our Saviour; That being justified by his grace, we should be made heirs according to the hope of eternal life" (Titus 3:5–7).

Chapter 12

Precepts of Men Titled: Hypocrites

The first precept ("You shall attend Mass on Sundays and holy days of obligation.")

The second precept ("You shall confess your sins at least once a year.")

The third precept ("You shall humbly receive your Creator in Holy Communion at least during the Easter season.")

The fourth precept ("You shall keep holy the holy days of obligation.")

The fifth precept ("You shall observe the prescribed days of fasting and abstinence.")
    The Catechism of the Catholic Church - 2042

"But in vain they do worship me, teaching for doctrines the commandments of men."

Matthew 15:9

God identifies those who teach the precepts of men as hypocrites. Essentially, what happened at the Council of Trent in 1545 was not an agreement to cease what is reprehensible to God—the pope's creation of man-made doctrine—but rather it dramatically advanced this practice. The pronouncement was made that, henceforth, these humanly-conceived doctrines were equal in authority to God's Word.

Evidence of our Lord's disdain for those pretenders declaring to have powers equal to His is found in both the Old and New Testaments, a sure sign of the seriousness of their deception.

"Ye hypocrites, well did Esaias prophesy of you, saying, This people draweth nigh unto me with their mouth, and honoureth me with their lips; but their heart is far from me. But in vain they do worship me, teaching for doctrines the commandments of men" (Matthew 15:7–9).

We must not be surprised that this same self-enlightened church hierarchy has not succeeded in duplicating God's other manifested power, the power of creation: no new heavens, universes, or a new earth. If they could produce new physical realms, then perhaps we could understand their claim to the right to pronounce doctrine, which they consider equal in authority with that of the Father and Son. But they don't have this right. They never did and they never will!

Nevertheless, over the centuries, the Vatican has continued to proclaim Catholic Tradition equal in authority to God's Word. No wonder the Creator, and soon-to-be Judge, describes such presumptuous men as "hypocrites."

Are you still comfortable believing that Catholic Tradition is necessary for salvation? If so, Satan has successfully clouded your mind by placing a veil between your eyes and the truth. The hypocrites have convinced you of your need for their self-serving, non-scriptural doctrine. Unfortunately, we must point out that according to God's inerrant Word, you are perishing! You are hell-bound and don't even know it!

"But if our gospel be hid, it is hid to them that are lost: In whom the god of this world hath blinded the minds of them which believe not, lest the light of the glorious gospel of Christ, who is the image of God, should shine unto them" (2nd Corinthians 4:3–4).

Most Catholics just cannot purge themselves of the need to do something in order to deserve salvation. Their church has filled this void by demanding lots of servitude. Performance toward satisfying this bondage is a massive dose of self-righteous pride.

God does not need our puny help! Yes, after we repent and accept Jesus Christ as our personal Savior and Lord, we are expected to strictly obey God's will. But His will is found only in the Bible.

Those who strive for complete obedience to God are manifesting a characteristic of a born again Christian. They are indwelt by the Holy Spirit and assuredly will be taken out of this world by Christ Himself to be with their Lord forever. The Word of God assures this. Regrettably, Catholic Tradition, ignores this "Blessed Hope," even though it's described in two books and spoken of, or alluded to in five other books of the Bible.

Unbelievers are often ashamed because they cannot contribute anything to God's gift. They want to make salvation complex when it's all so simple for those who possess a childlike faith.

My unwavering Catholic faith conditioned me to believe that I needed their complicated system that leads to salvation. The most tragic aspect of this is that not a single Catholic is certain of their salvation. This also applies to the pope, cardinals, bishops, priests, or nuns. They can't experience the blessed assurance of salvation that comes from a simple childlike faith in the Gospel of Jesus Christ! Their church teaches the need for works, but doesn't know how many works are needed for salvation. The Bible teaches otherwise.

"For I am not ashamed of the gospel of Christ: for it is the power of God unto salvation to every one that believeth; to the Jew first, and also to the Greek. For therein is the righteousness of God revealed from faith to faith: as it is written, The just shall live by faith" (Romans 1:16–17).

"And I give unto them eternal life; and they shall never perish, neither shall any man pluck them out of my hand. My Father, which gave them me, is greater than all; and no man is able to pluck them out of my Father's hand. I and my Father are one" (John 10:28–30).

"These things have I written unto you that believe on the name of the Son of God; that ye may know that ye have eternal life, and that ye may believe on the name of the Son of God" (1st John 5:13).

Chapter 13

Evil Men

"The Roman Pontiff, head of the college of bishops, enjoys this infallibility in virtue of his office, when, as supreme pastor and teacher of all of the faithful - who confirms his brethren in the faith - he proclaims by a definitive act a doctrine pertaining to faith or morals...The infallibility promised to the Church is also present in the body of bishops when, together with Peter's successor, they exercise the supreme Magisterium," above all in an Ecumenical Council. When the Church through its supreme Magisterium proposes as doctrine "for belief as being divinely revealed," and as the teaching of Christ, the definitions "must be adhered to with the obedience of faith." This infallibility extends as far as the deposit of divine Revelation itself."

The Catechism of the Catholic Church - 891

"*For other foundation can no man lay than that is laid, which is Jesus Christ.*"

1ˢᵗ Corinthians 3:11

Dave Hunt, arguably one of the foremost evangelical writers concerning the history and current condition of the Roman Catholic Church, made some comments at a Bible prophecy conference in Atlanta.[1]

Asked during a question-and-answer session of the conference whether he thought the false prophet during the tribulation period in the book of Revelation would be the current pope, John Paul II, or a future pope, Hunt replied: "Any answer, of course, is speculation: I believe a pope will be the false prophet."

He followed up with specific reasons to lend credence to his opinion, and expressed several times that some of the popes "...were the worst monsters that ever walked the face of the earth."

Since I had read his book, *A Woman Rides the Beast* several times, I was not at all surprised by his statements. However, one of his comments, however, was new to me. He related that Pope John IX worshipped Satan at the altar of St. Peter in the Vatican. Other reputable writers have reported similar incidents of Satan worship in the Vatican. One such account is documented later in this book.

Those who have neither read Hunt's book nor heard any of his tapes will probably be shocked by these statements as well as some of the other revelations disclosed in Atlanta. You will not be shocked, however, if you study the history of the Catholic Church. However, one excellent way to get an overview is to write or call for *The Kingdom of Blood* audio briefing package prepared by Koinonia House. This contains two audio tapes, plus written notes. Each tape is approximately one hour in length. The first is by Chuck Missler and the second by Dave Hunt, who summarizes his own book, *A Woman Rides the Beast*.[2]

Vatican intrigues also involve very recent history; for example; the alleged murder of the current pope's predecessor, Pope John Paul I.

If you are interested, obtain the book, *In God's Name: An Investigation Into the Murder Of Pope John Paul I* by David Yallop, an investigative reporter who spent three years documenting the alleged murder.

Yallop doesn't doubt that John Paul I was indeed murdered. He reports that the newly elected John Paul I was preparing to "clean house" not only in the Vatican but also throughout the church's far-reaching power centers including the U.S.A.

Unfortunately, a cadre of evil lieutenants allegedly put an end to the pope's aspirations. He died after serving just 33 days in office. Interestingly, Jesus Christ lived just 33 years before the evil men of His day murdered Him. Often Scripture relates days to years and years to days. Maybe this event is a coincidence, maybe not.

Just prior to his execution by Emperor Nero, one of the most evil men in history, the apostle Paul wrote a letter to one of his most beloved believers, Timothy. This epistle was written about A.D. 65–66 and is called the second epistle to Timothy.

Timothy, an elder in the church of Ephesus, was besieged by brethren who had entered the Church with false doctrine and who wanted to improve on or alter this gift of God's perfect love.

In his letter, Paul counsels and encourages Timothy to retain the basic teachings of Scripture which are perfect, complete and eternally sufficient. Paul also points to the future when men will hear only what they want to hear rather than listening exclusively to God's Word: *"All scripture is given by inspiration of God, and is profitable for doctrine, for reproof, for correction, for instruction in righteousness"* (2nd Timothy 3:16).

"For the time will come when they will not endure sound doctrine; but after their own lusts shall they heap to themselves teachers, having itching ears; And they shall turn away their ears from the truth, and shall be turned unto fables" (2nd Timothy 4:3–4).

Men have promoted chaos within the Christian community right from the very beginning of the early Church because they have wanted their ideas to be equal with those of God the Father and God the Son. They have been inspired by Satan, the ruler of this world, to write doctrine which they declare infallible. The apostle Paul undoubtedly had the apostate church in mind when he wrote, *"...And they shall turn away their ears from the truth, and shall be turned unto fables."* He exhorted Timothy to simply preach the Word.

During my early years as a Catholic, I never thought I would ever say that doctrines crafted by the Catholic Church were myths. I now have no doubt, but rather peace of mind that they are myths because there is no basis in God's Word for the false doctrines created by the Church of Rome. Second Timothy 3:1 says: *"This know also, that in the last days perilous times shall come."*

If you study the Bible thoroughly you will realize that we are in the last days right now. Paul describes the condition of the times we live in: *"Yea, and all that will live godly in Christ Jesus shall suffer persecution. But evil men and seducers shall wax worse and worse, deceiving, and being deceived"* (2nd Timothy 3:12–13).

How much wrath has God stored up for these unbelievers? Read the book of Revelation and find out.

Remember, however, that the Body of Christ, His Church, will not be involved during the horrific events depicted in the book of Revelation.

The Catholic Church has successfully projected an image of godliness. But its message is one that demands an allegiance to unbiblical doctrines. The Bible warns that we should avoid such men as these. *"Having a form of godliness, but denying the power thereof: from such turn away"* (2nd Timothy 3:5).

The apostle John, granted a view of the endtimes, wrote that he heard a voice coming down from heaven, a command to abandon the apostate church which most Bible scholars identify as "Babylon the Great" described in the book of Revelation. *"And I heard another voice from heaven, saying, Come out of her, my people, that ye be not partakers of her sins, and that ye receive not of her plagues"* (Revelation 18:4).

[1]Dave Hunt, Audiotape 7 B, *Atlanta Prophecy Conference 1997*, Midnight Call Ministries, P.O. Box 280008, Columbia, SC 29228

[2]*The Kingdom of Blood* audio briefing package
Koinonia House , P.O. Box D, Coeur d'Alene, ID 83816–0347

Chapter 14

The Evil Team: The "Dragon," The "Beast," The "False Prophet"

If anyone says that justifying faith is nothing else than confidence in divine mercy which remits sins for Christ's sake, or that it is the confidence alone that justifies us, let him be anathema.

Council of Trent - Canon 12

"Verily, verily I say unto you, He that heareth my word, and believeth on him that sent me, hath everlasting life, and shall not come into condemnation: but is passed from death unto life."

John 5:24

Lucifer, the most magnificent and powerful of the fallen angelic host, has another biblical name: Satan. His name means "adversary," and he is the adversary of God's Son, Jesus Christ. Satan is also described as the "dragon," the "devil" and the "ruler of this world." Some translations use "prince of this world."

"Now is the judgment of this world: now shall the prince of this world be cast out" (John 12:31).

"Of judgment, because the prince of this world is judged" (John 16:11).

The Bible also informs us that Satan has the authority and power to give all the kingdoms of this world to the Son of God, or for that matter, to anyone he so chooses.

"And the devil, taking him up into an high mountain, shewed unto him all the kingdoms of the world in a moment of time. And the devil said unto him, All this power will I give thee, and the glory of them: for that is delivered unto me; and to whomsoever I will I give it. If thou therefore wilt worship me, all shall be thine. And Jesus answered and said unto him, Get thee behind me, Satan: for it is written, Thou shalt worship the Lord thy God, and him only shalt thou serve" (Luke 4:5–8).

With these passages in mind, the reader should not be surprised to find that Satan will turn over total world dominion to the Antichrist whom the Bible refers to as the "beast."

The forthcoming world leader, Antichrist/beast will not be able to accomplish his remarkable deeds through humanly-restricted abilities. He will be supernaturally empowered by Satan! But thankfully, Satan cannot yet transfer his supernatural capabilities to the Antichrist/beast because the Holy Spirit is still shepherding the Body of Christ (His Church) here on earth.

The Holy Spirit is restraining Satan from doing everything he would like to do. The Body of Christ and the Holy

Spirit will depart this earth with Christ before the identity of the Antichrist becomes known and established. Because of its overwhelming importance, I'll once again provide a description of the Body of Christ: Those who have accepted Christ's shed blood as the exclusive reason for salvation.

"For by grace are ye saved through faith; and that not of yourselves: it is the gift of God: Not of works, lest any man should boast" (Ephesians 2:8–9).

Becoming part of the Body of Christ, His Church, means that you will be taken off this earth before the Antichrist is revealed! So you will be in heaven with your personal Savior and you will enjoy the Marriage Supper of the Lamb. All believers saved throughout time, will become the Bride of Christ. No celebration throughout history, no matter how elaborate, can be compared to the joy of participating in the Marriage Supper of the Lamb.

"Let us be glad and rejoice, and give honour to him: for the marriage of the Lamb is come, and his wife hath made herself ready" (Revelation 19:7).

"And he saith unto me, Write, Blessed are they which are called unto the marriage supper of the Lamb. And he saith unto me, These are the true sayings of God" (Revelation 19:9).

Those of us who are saved will come back with Jesus after the Great Tribulation to rule with Him over those who are still living on earth during the 1,000-year Millennium. This is known as the Second Coming of Christ.

There will not be as many people populating the earth as there are today. The Bible indicates that two-thirds of the world's population will be killed during the Great Tribulation. We will be with Christ during His 1,000-year reign, and we, as His Body will remain with our Lord and Savior forever.

All those unsaved throughout the centuries will be condemned to eternal punishment at the Great White Throne Judgment. This includes those who did not accept Christ during the tribulation.

Catholicism recognizes and expounds from the pulpit about the great eternal dangers of being part of the Great White Throne Judgment.

However, rarely, if ever, do Catholics hear about the Judgment Seat of Jesus Christ. Since only believers are found at this event, this silence is understandable. Catholics don't know whether they are saved until after their death; therefore, when they die, most Catholics must appear at the Great White Throne Judgment. Of course, this also applies to all others, regardless of church membership or religion. Eternal life is only available through Christ; without Him, there is none.

Believers know they are immediately saved upon receiving Jesus Christ as personal Savior and Lord over their lives. The believer's life is evaluated by his Savior. This occurs immediately following the Rapture of the Body.

Believers are never condemned to eternal punishment at the Judgment Seat of Christ, but rather they are rewarded for their good deeds. Good deeds will produce eternal value, while all other deeds will be burned up. Again, the important aspects to remember about judgment are:

1) The Judgment Seat of Christ is reserved for believers only.

2) Not a single believer will appear at the Great White Throne Judgment.

Paul speaks to believers in the following Scripture: *"For we must all appear before the judgment seat of Christ; that every one may receive the things done in his body, according to that he hath done, whether it be good or bad"* (2nd Corinthians 5:10).

Those who are not believers, and therefore not raptured, will suffer through the tribulation, the second three and a half years of which will be the most devastating period in the entire history of mankind!

It is important to note that people can be saved during the tribulation period. However, many will die before they have the chance to repent and receive Jesus as personal Savior due to natural calamities Scripture says will be severe and numerous. That's why most Bible scholars believe that few Gentiles will be saved during the tribulation period. The opportunities for Gentiles to be saved is at hand now during the "time of the Gentiles." God is primarily dealing with the Jews during the tribulation period:

"For then shall be great tribulation, such as was not since the beginning of the world to this time, no, nor ever shall be. And except those days should be shortened, there should no flesh be saved: but for the elect's sake those days shall be shortened" (Matthew 24:21–22).

Dear reader, please repent of your sins and sincerely ask Jesus Christ into your heart as personal Savior and Lord of your life. Do this now, if you have not already done so.

Tell Him that you surrender your life and heart to Him.

Doing His will, and not your own is the most important goal of your life. If you do this with complete sincerity, you can be sure that you will participate at the Judgment Seat of Christ. You will not endure the Great Tribulation, or the condemning Great White Throne Judgment. Nothing in His Word indicates that man-made doctrines and traditions are necessary to accomplish His goal for you, which is eternal security!

Long ago, the Catholic Church created and adapted the concept of "purgatory," which in part was derived from the apocryphal book of Second Maccabees 12:39–45.

This doctrine was elevated to dogma status at the Council of Florence in 1438. Although this philosophical creation cannot be found in the Holy Scriptures, it has been carried down through the centuries as part of Catholic Tradition. From 1438 until today, this dogma has been an eternally binding yoke of bondage for every faithful Catholic.

The Vatican wants us to believe that Catholic Tradition was inspired by the Holy Spirit of God. Jesus Christ states that such tradition invalidates His own Word. *"Making the word of God of none effect through your tradition, which ye have delivered: and many such like things do ye"* (Mark 7:13).

Critics of accepting Jesus Christ as Savior in order to be assured of eternal security have called this a "silver bullet." Those contemptuous of this clearly biblical tenet say, "It's just too simple! God wants you to do works for salvation!" God detests those critics because they are defying His Word.

Let's zero in on this issue: We don't need a debate among theologians to determine that those critics are telling God that He is a liar. Throughout His instruction book, God states that salvation is achieved only through His Son. It says nothing about supplementing trust in the Son with works. Nothing!

"For God so loved the world, that he gave his only begotten Son, that whosoever believeth in him should not perish, but have everlasting life" (John 3:16).

Go back to the beginning of this book and re-read what the *Catechism of the Catholic Church* states on page 37; #136 declares:

> "God is the author of Sacred Scripture because he inspired its
> human authors; he acts in them and by means of them. He
> thus gives assurance that their writings teach without error
> his saving truth."

How can one billion Catholics world-wide accept this when almost the entirety of Catholicism today is based not on Sacred Scripture, but on Catholic Tradition? Virtually all Catholic Tradition directly conflicts with Sacred Scripture, the same Sacred Scripture which the Catechism claims to be "teachings without error." The Vatican has been misleading their followers for centuries in an unbroken chain to this day!

Who is to blame? Catholics! In most cases, they unwittingly have not turned away from this deception! As mentioned before, some Catholics are part of the Body of Christ. But I am desperately worried about those who continue to let the true Gospel be veiled and who are perishing.

If you're saying, "I don't think it's happening to me," then be warned that if you're not sure, then it probably is happening to you.

Are you perishing? Yes, likely you are if you do not exclusively obey what the Son says. You must stop obeying the precepts of men. *"He that believeth on the Son hath everlasting life: and he that believeth not the Son shall not see life; but the wrath of God abideth on him"* (John 3:36).

Chapter 15

Could The Pope Be The False Prophet?

Consequently we declare, state, define, and pronounce that it is altogether necessary to salvation for every creature to be subject to the Roman Pontiff.

Unam Sanctum, Pope Boniface, - November 18, 1302

"For there is one God, and one mediator between God and men, the man Christ Jesus."

1st Timothy 2:5

"Beware of false prophets, which come to you in sheep's clothing, but inwardly they are ravening wolves."

Matthew 7:15

The dragon we read about in the book of Revelation is the devil; the fallen angel, Lucifer.

The beast is the soon-coming world dictator, the Antichrist.

But we need further information about the third member of the evil team, the false prophet. Dave Hunt states that the false prophet will be a pope. He is not the only biblical commentator who has come to that conclusion.

As the Antichrist's right hand man, the false prophet will assuredly be the head of the politically correct one-world religion of the last days.

It is not hard to put two and two together. Pope John Paul II has not veiled his intentions to lead the Ecumenical Movement, the process prophesied to conclude with the formation of a single global religion. In fact, most modern popes have been ecumenically active.

"As further proof of the ecumenism of John Paul II's immediate predecessors, Paul VI gave his blessing to the Second World Conference on Religion and Peace in Louvain, Belgium, in 1974. Under Catholic leadership, the Louvain Declaration stated:

"Buddhists, Christians, Confucianists, Hindus, Jains, Jews, Muslims, Shintoists, Sikhs, Zoroastrians and still others, we have sought here to listen to the spirit within our varied and venerable religious traditions...we have grappled with the towering issues that our societies must resolve in order to bring about peace...We rejoice that...the long era of prideful and even prejudiced isolation of the religions of humanity is, we hope, now gone forever."[1]

The above participants, with the exception of true Christians, don't recognize Jesus Christ as God, and they certainly don't believe in the Gospel of Jesus Christ.

Although Jews don't accept Christ, they do believe in God the Father as found in the Old Testament. Most Jews would probably be ashamed to know that representatives of their faith participated in the Louvain conference.

Nevertheless, the conference was just one of the earlier affirmations of the Vatican's agenda. It was designed to promote and control the process leading to a global religion. Most Bible scholars anticipate the soon advent of a single world religion to be a confederation shaped by some form of Christianity and paganism. Additionally it will embrace everything that is politically correct.

So we see a Roman Catholic organization today not primarily oriented to preaching the Gospel of Jesus Christ.

Rather, Rome wants to embrace every religion imaginable and lead them into a one-world spiritual family. That is a politically correct strategy which makes a great deal of sense when the goal is to establish the pope as the world's religious leader.

I'll add my name to those who believe that a pope will be the false prophet! Read on and you'll see why. Probably not the current pontiff, John Paul II, but his immediate successor may well be the one chosen by the Cardinals, but permitted by God. Oh yes, it will be accomplished by God's hand! He has maintained total control over every event of history; past, present and future. He scrupulously sees to it that His Word comes to pass exactly as it is written!

Malachi Martin provides insight and perspective on this topic in the June 10, 1996 edition of *U.S. News & World Report*, Martin was interviewed about *Windswept House*, his fictional work of the naming of the successor to John Paul II. He commented:

Question: "Your novel depicts an international plot by

Vatican insiders and internationalists to install a new pope and establish a 'New World Order.' How fictional is this story line?"

Answer: "Not very. There is an unspoken alliance today between powers inside the Vatican and leaders of major international humanist organizations who would change the Roman Catholic Church from a sacred institution to one whose primary function is to act as a stabilizing social force in the world. The Roman church is the only global structure able to do this. The one obstacle is John Paul II. He is seen as a defender of medieval traditions. They want a pope who shares their more liberal, globalist view."

Question: "Who are these powers?"

Answer: "Cardinals of the church; the men who will elect the next pope. I describe them as conciliarists. The church today is divided. Monolithic faith is gone. The new rival factions: traditionalists who prefer the church as it was before the reforms of the Second Vatican Council and conciliarists who want to liberalize church doctrine on everything from divorce and contraception to abortion and homosexuality. The numbers are about even, but the conciliarists hold the positions of power. They think John Paul II is too conservative; traditionalists don't think he is conservative enough."

Question: "What about the nonchurch part of the alliance? Who are they?"

Answer: "Academia, foundations, non-governmental organizations, even some governmental agencies. They have vast resources devoted to population control, education and economic and social stabilization. If they can get the Roman Catholic Church to side with them in the social and cultural field in a world that is dysfunctional, they'll have another element of stability."

Question: "This sounds rather conspiratorial."
Answer: "It's not a conspiracy, but it's deliberate.
Conciliarists and non-church globalists think the same way.
Neither like the pope's policies. They are preparing for the
selection of the next pope." [2]

The prophecies of Daniel, written 2,500 years ago, and
those of the apostle John in the book of Revelation almost
2,000 years ago are taking place before our very eyes. We
are in the last days!

There will be a one-world government, one currency, and
one religion. Circumstances indicate the strong possibility
that a pope will be in charge of the one-world religion, and
will establish himself as a key partner on the evil team. He
could very likely be the false prophet.

Over the years, the Catholic Church has fallen far from
the Gospel of Jesus Christ, which constituted the early
Church's only teaching. They have added numerous man-
made precepts and continue to further liberalize their anti-
biblical Catholic Tradition.

[1]Dave Hunt, *A Woman Rides The Beast*, 1994, Harvest House
Publishers, p.422–23

[2]*U.S. News & World Report*, June 10, 1996

Chapter 16

Modern Israel: A Sign That The Church Will Depart Soon

And when one considers the future, God's People of the Old Covenant and the new People of God tend towards similar goals: expectation of the coming (or the return) of the Messiah. But one awaits the return of the Messiah who died and rose from the dead and is recognized as Lord and Son of God; the other awaits the coming of a Messiah, whose features remain hidden till the end of time; and the latter waiting is accompanied by the drama of not knowing or of misunderstanding Christ Jesus.

The Catechism of the Catholic Church - 840

"...and when we shall see him, there is no beauty that we should desire him. He is despised and rejected of men; a man of sorrows, and acquainted with grief: and we hid as it were our faces from him; he was despised, and we esteemed him not...But he was wounded for our transgressions, he was bruised for our iniquities: the chastisement of our peace was upon him; and with his stripes we are healed."

Isaiah 53:2-3,5

Nothing in the Bible suggests that the Rapture, the departing of the Holy Spirit and the Body of Christ, cannot occur at any moment. Rather, the Bible surely details that we are in the general time period when this "Blessed Hope" for believers will take place.

Until 1948, the immanency of this event was not possible since Israel had not yet become a nation. Since 1948, Israel has attracted Jews, scattered about the world, back to where God has wanted them to be. This event has marked the beginning of the last days. Catholic pulpits and many Protestant pulpits remained silent about the importance of the nation of Israel in God's inalterable plans.

Some early Church Fathers, notably Aquinas and Augustine assumed that when the Jews killed Christ, they forfeited God's promises which were then transferred to the Church. The Roman Catholic Church has embraced these unbiblical teachings and continues to cling steadfastly to them.

This is one of the earliest examples of the precepts of men usurping the Word of God. What the Bible says is what the Bible means, and it says that God has special plans for the Jews. God's Word never changes. *"Heaven and earth shall pass away, but my words shall not pass away"* (Matthew 24:35). Everything God has said will be accomplished for the nation of Israel: He is still in charge!

Every capital in the world today is concerned with the events in Israel, particularly Jerusalem. An Old Testament prophet wrote 2,500 years ago: *"Behold, I will make Jerusalem a cup of trembling unto all the people round about, when they shall be in the siege both against Judah and against Jerusalem"* (Zechariah 12:2).

Notice the words of Zechariah: *"against Judah."* That means against God's chosen people, the nation of Israel. Those not raptured will see first-hand how God's chosen people will be spared from eternal condemnation. God will pour out *"the spirit of grace."* The Jews will be saved! Aquinas and Augustine, their Catholic followers, and some Protestants will be proven wrong.

"And it shall come to pass in that day, that I will seek to destroy all the nations that come against Jerusalem. And I will pour upon the house of David, and upon the inhabitants of Jerusalem, the spirit of grace and of supplications: and they shall look upon me whom they have pierced, and they shall mourn for him, as one mourneth for his only son, and shall be in bitterness for him, as one that is in bitterness for his firstborn" (Zechariah 12: 9–10).

"And at that time shall Michael stand up, the great prince which standeth for the children of thy people: and there shall be a time of trouble, such as never was since there was a nation even to that same time: and at that time thy people shall be delivered, every one that shall be found written in the book. And many of them that sleep in the dust of the earth shall awake, some to everlasting life, and some to shame and everlasting contempt. And they that be wise shall shine as the brightness of the firmament; and they that turn many to righteousness as the stars for ever and ever. But thou, O Daniel, shut up the words, and seal the book, even to the time of the end: many shall run to and fro, and knowledge shall be increased" (Daniel 12:1–4).

If you are not sure of your own eternal security and refuse the insight of Daniel chapter 12, then you would do well to consider what Jesus Himself said in answer to His apostle's question, *"Why speakest thou unto them in parables?"* (Matthew 13:10).

"He answered and said unto them, Because it is given unto you to know the mysteries of the kingdom of heaven, but to them it is not given. For whosoever hath, to him shall be given, and he shall have more abundance: but whosoever

hath not, from him shall be taken away even that he hath.
Therefore speak I to them in parables: because they seeing
see not; and hearing they hear not, neither do they under-
stand. And in them is fulfilled the prophecy of Esaias, which
saith, By hearing ye shall hear, and shall not understand;
and seeing ye shall see, and shall not perceive: For this peo-
ple's heart is waxed gross, and their ears are dull of hear-
ing, and their eyes they have closed; lest at any time they
should see with their eyes, and hear with their ears, and
should understand with their heart, and should be con-
verted, and I should heal them" (Matthew 13:11–15).

Oh, how important this message must be to Jesus Christ
and therefore to all of us! In addition to its appearance in
Isaiah and Matthew, it also appears in the book of Acts. If
you insist on following the precepts of men rather than the
Word of God, then you are the target of this message. This
is truly a word to the wise! If you don't accept it, you don't
have the insight of Daniel 12:3. And, now, an additional
thought about the future if you should continue to adhere to
the precepts of men instead of the Word of God: *"And for*
this cause God shall send them strong delusion, that they
should believe a lie" (2nd Thessalonians 2:11).

Chapter 17

Are You An Idolater?

"We pronounce, declare, and define it to be a divinely revealed dogma: that the Immaculate Mother of God, the ever Virgin Mary, having completed the course of her earthly life, was assumed body and soul into heavenly glory. Hence, if anyone, which God forbid, should dare wilfully to deny or call into doubt that which we have defined, let him know that he has completely fallen from the divine and Catholic faith...It is forbidden to any man to change this, Our declaration, pronouncement, and definition or, by rash attempt, to oppose and counter it. If any man should presume to make such an attempt, let him know that he will incur the wrath of Almighty God and of the Blessed Apostles Peter and Paul.

Taken from Selected Documents of Pope Pius XII
1950 A.D.

"*As it is written, There is none righteous, no, not one...For all have sinned, and come short of the glory of God.*"

Romans 3:10, 23

Webster's New Collegiate Dictionary defines an idolater as "a worshiper of idols." Most Bible-believing theologians believe that practicing Catholics are idolaters. But individual Catholics will vehemently protest this accusation.

Let's consider another word, "Mariology," which is defined as excessive veneration of the virgin Mary. Again, we bring common sense into play as we attempt to discern the truth. Is Mariology, in addition to saint imaging and worship, intended by God, or is it simply a creative idea promulgated by men?

During the first 500 years following the death of Jesus Christ, the Christian Church neither venerated Mary nor any other saints. Most all historians agree on this issue.

Dr. J. M. Carroll and others point out that Mariology did not become endemic to the Catholic Church until the fifth century, while general saint and image worship did not become endemic until almost the eighth century.[1]

Clearly, idol worship was not condoned by the early Church Fathers. It was a man-made idea primarily spread by the Catholic apostate movement of the early Christian Church. The followers of true Christianity continued to be governed by the warnings of the prophets. For instance, through Isaiah, God said: *"I am the LORD: that is my name: and my glory will I not give to another, neither my praise to graven images"* (Isaiah 42:8). These words are plain and designate no exception, not even for Jesus' earthly mother.

Rather, Jesus Christ respected His mother for doing only what He expects you and me to do: Hear and obey His Word. He reckons you and me as equals with His mother if we do just that. No Scripture even remotely commands us to venerate the human mother of Jesus Christ.

When reflecting on this, always remember that Christ existed before Mary was born: *"In the beginning was the Word, and the Word was with God, and the Word was*

God" (John 1:1). In this instance "Word" is another biblical name for Jesus.

"And it was told him by certain which said, Thy mother and thy brethren stand without, desiring to see thee. And he answered and said unto them, My mother and my brethren are these which hear the word of God, and do it" (Luke 8:20–21).

Scripture makes it clear that many of the claims by the Vatican for Mary are preposterous and contrary to the Word of God! All veneration of Mary is, at best, idol and image worship.

Later in this book, I will point out that Pope Sixtus (1585–90) took it upon himself to rewrite the Bible to his own liking, a work quickly transformed back to its near original form by church scholars immediately upon his death. Pretty incredible? Yes! But not as deceitful as this next Vatican alteration of the Word of God, which is directly related to their insistence on promoting idol and image veneration.

The Roman Catholic Church, in order to draw attention away from God's contempt for idol worship, has eliminated one of His Ten Commandments. Pages 496–497 of *The Catechism of the Catholic Church* lists the Ten Commandments. Under the heading: "A Traditional Catechetical Formula," the second commandment, reads as follows:

"You shall not take the name of the Lord your God in vain."

The "Traditional Catechetical Formula" lists the third commandment as the second commandment, effectively eliminating the second commandment! The men of the Vatican have once again attempted to overrule Almighty God! When you read the second commandment as put forth in Exodus 20 and Deuteronomy 5, the reason becomes abundantly clear:

"Thou shalt not make unto thee any graven image, or any likeness of any thing that is in heaven above, or that is in the earth beneath, or that is in the water under the earth: Thou shalt not bow down thyself to them, nor serve them: for I the LORD thy God am a jealous God, visiting the iniquity of the fathers upon the children unto the third and fourth generation of them that hate me; And shewing mercy unto thousands of them that love me, and keep my commandments" (Exodus 20:4–6).

Thou shalt not make thee any graven image, or any likeness of any thing that is in heaven above, or that is in the earth beneath, or that is in the waters beneath the earth: Thou shalt not bow down thyself unto them, nor serve them: for I the LORD thy God am a jealous God, visiting the iniquity of the fathers upon the children unto the third and fourth generation of them that hate me, And shewing mercy unto thousands of them that love me and keep my commandments" (Deuteronomy 5:8–10).

It can't be any clearer than that: any adoration, honor, or exaltation of Mary and other saints is an abomination to God. Any statue, shrine or other graven image made in the likeness of anyone for the purpose of worship or veneration is condemned by the Father.

The Catholic Church has slapped God in the face by eliminating one of His commandments. We can also infer from the above that not obeying and venerating only Him is choosing to venerate others. Even third and fourth-generation children will be affected by this sin. This should call for serious reflection by practicing Catholics.

You may have been thinking, "If Rome has eliminated one of the commandments, do they now recognize only nine?" No. They have expanded the tenth commandment to become the new ninth and tenth commandments. Number nine: You shall not covet thy neighbor's wife. Number ten:

You shall not covet thy neighbor's goods. Exodus and Deuteronomy are combined into the tenth commandment. Apparently the mere mortals in the Vatican know better than God!

[1]Dr. J.M. Carroll, *The Trail of Blood*, 1931, Ashland Baptist Church.

Chapter 18

Catholic Clergy and Eternity

As in the case of Baptism and Confirmation this share in Christ's office is granted once for all. The sacrament of Holy Orders, like the other two, confers an *indellible spiritual character* and cannot be repeated or conferred temporarily.

It is true that someone validly ordained can, for a just reason, be discharged from the obligations and functions linked to ordination, or can be forbidden to exercise them; but he cannot become a laymen again in the strict sense, because the character imprinted by ordination is for ever.

The Catechism of the Catholic Church - 1582, 1583

"And hath made us kings and priests unto God and his Father: to him be glory and dominion for ever and ever. Amen"

Revelation 1:6

Catholic readers who have digested the material in this book up to this point may raise the question about whether Catholic clergy are guilty of deception. Since we have already established that Scripture directly contradicts the teaching that Catholic Tradition has equal authority with Scripture, we can assume that most priests, nuns, bishops, cardinals and popes have indeed been deceiving the faithful. Most seem to be ignorant of the discord between biblical teachings and Catholic Tradition.

The Catechism of the Catholic Church makes it abundantly clear that Scripture is from God, but the Catechism also reveals:

> "It is clear therefore that, in the supremely wise arrangement of God, sacred Tradition, Sacred Scripture, and the Magisterium of the Church are so connected and associated that one of them cannot stand without the others. Working together, each in its own way, under the action of the Holy Spirit, they all contribute effectively to the salvation of souls." #95, P. 29

Of course, Catholic clergy justify what they teach based on those beliefs. However, there is no justification, as Scripture clearly proclaims that Tradition and the need for the Magisterium are counter to the Word of God. "The supremely wise arrangement of God" is not found in Scripture — it's from the imagination of men.

"Howbeit in vain do they worship me, teaching for doctrines the commandments of men. For laying aside the commandment of God, ye hold the tradition of men, as the washing of pots and cups: and many other such like things ye do. And he said unto them, Full well ye reject the commandment of God, that ye may keep your own tradition" (Mark 7:7–9).

*"Making the word of God of none effect through your tra-
dition, which ye have delivered: and many such like things
do ye"* (Mark 7:13).

Those Scriptures are straightforward. Catholic clergy
must all be in a haze by not realizing they are indeed preaching the precepts of men! The Magisterium is nothing more
than the result of a self-proclaimed right to interpret God's
Word for others. God's Word proclaims that each and every
one of us should read the Bible daily.

*"These were more noble than those in Thessalonica, in
that they received the word with all readiness of mind, and
searched the scriptures daily, whether those things were so"*
(Acts 17:11).

Nothing in Scripture even hints of the need for a special
body of men to interpret the Bible. This holds true for
Protestants as well as Catholics. Many Protestant churches
have gifted speakers, but each member of every congregation must look to the Bible personally to see if everything
seen and heard is totally consistent with the Bible.

One must wonder where the Holy Spirit was for the first
fifteen centuries after the death of Jesus Christ. Not until the
Council of Trent in 1545, did the Catholic Church officially
claim that Tradition was equal in authority to Scripture.

The Vatican has written in their Catechism that the
Bible cannot stand alone without being connected with
man-made doctrines thought up many centuries after the
Savior's death.

Also, the faithful must trust the judgment of the
Magisterium for all biblical interpretations. This is certainly
understandable because it's quite evident they don't want
their members to really know the truth of God's Word.

The most important element to understand is that
Catholic Tradition is comprised of purely self-conceived
precepts labeled as infallible. History tells us that popes

have ruled infallible doctrines of previous popes as hereti-
cal and rescinded them. How then could the original ver-
sions have been infallible?

My own assessment, backed by 64 years of experience,
stands: Many leaders at all levels of the Catholic clergy have
been deceiving the Catholic faithful. They will each be
judged by the Person whose Word they have corrupted.
Many have done this unwittingly and only God knows their
heart. But those who have done so knowingly and don't
repent have no hope of salvation.

Chapter 19

The Bible or Tradition?

"Sacred Tradition and Sacred Scripture, then, are bound closely together and communicate one with the other. For both of them, flowing out from the same divine well-spring, come together in some fashion to form one thing and move towards the same goal." Each of them makes present and fruitful in the Church the mystery of Christ, who promised to remain with his own "always, to the close of the age."

The Catechism of the Catholic Church - 80

"Forasmuch as ye know that ye were not redeemed with corruptible things, as silver and gold, from your vain conversation received by tradition from your fathers."

1ˢᵗ Peter 1:18

Now that we have seen what the Catholic Church has said, let's see what the Bible says about those who teach the man-made concept of tradition. It is hard to escape what the Holy Spirit declares in Mark's gospel account: *"...Full well ye reject the commandment of God, that ye may keep your own tradition"* (Mark 7:9).

Was Mark, in part, prophesying that *The Catechism of the Catholic Church* would set aside God's second commandment in order to keep its tradition of idol worship?

It is very important to point out that the following Scripture written by the apostle Paul is directed only to the born again Christian. If you are not born again, and are following non-scriptural teachings, you are believing in the "spirit of the world." Catholic clergy are guilty of teaching the "spirit of the world," the precepts of men, rather than the Word of God.

"Now we have received, not the spirit of the world, but the spirit which is of God; that we might know the things that are freely given to us of God. Which things also we speak, not in the words which man's wisdom teacheth, but which the Holy Ghost teacheth; comparing spiritual things with spiritual. But the natural man receiveth not the things of the Spirit of God: for they are foolishness unto him: neither can he know them, because they are spiritually discerned. But he that is spiritual judgeth all things, yet he himself is judged of no man. For who hath known the mind of the Lord, that he may instruct him? But we have the mind of Christ" (1st Corinthians 2:12–16).

If you read that Scripture again and again, you will have very little room to believe that Catholic Tradition is anything less than a violation of God's Word. God wants us to believe in His Word and His Word only, the Bible. Catholic Tradition is overwhelmingly oriented to *additions* to Holy Scripture. Scripture surely warns those who add to His Word:

"Add thou not unto his words, lest he reprove thee, and thou be found a liar" (Proverbs 30:6).

I'll conclude this with a scriptural message to those who practice the lawlessness of teaching unbiblical doctrine:

"Not every one that saith unto me, Lord, Lord, shall enter into the kingdom of heaven; but he that doeth the will of my Father which is in heaven. Many will say to me in that day, Lord, Lord, have we not prophesied in thy name? and in thy name have cast out devils? and in thy name done many wonderful works? And then will I profess unto them, I never knew you: depart from me, ye that work iniquity" (Matthew 7:21–23).

Final disposition of individual members of Catholic leadership can once again be summed up by Jesus' answer to Nicodemus, a leading Jewish religious ruler of His day:

"...Verily, verily, I say unto thee, Except a man be born again, he cannot see the kingdom of God" (John 3:3).

Individual clerics must have a born again experience, just like you and me, in order to be saved. However, it is my own belief that God will cloud their minds and hearts to this need if they knowingly persist in teaching unbiblical precepts.

I have also observed that most Catholic clergy who have come to know the truth and are born again, promptly leave the apostate church.

Chapter 20

Satan Working Through The Church

Certain things are required in order to respond adequately to this call [of unity]:

- a permanent *renewal* of the Church is greater fidelity to her vocation; such renewal is the driving-force of the movement toward unity;

- *conversion of heart*, as the faithful "try to live holier lives according to the Gospel"; "for it is the unfaithfulness of the members of Christ's gift which causes divisions;

- *prayer in common*, because "change of heart and holiness of life, along with public and private prayer for the unity of Christians, should be regarded as the soul of the whole ecumenical movement, and merits the name 'spiritual ecumenism;'"

- *fraternal knowledge of each other*;

- *ecumenical formation* of the faithful and especially of priests;

- *dialogue* among theologians and meetings among Christians of the different churches and communities;

- *collaboration* among Christians in various areas of service to mankind. Human service is the idiomatic phrase.

The Catechism of the Catholic Church - 821

"Jesus saith unto him, I am the way, the truth, and the life; no man cometh unto the Father but by me."

John 14:6

Most Christians sadly underestimate the influence of Satan in their lives. He is the most powerful being on this planet. Of course, he is not even remotely as powerful as God the Father who created him, God the Son who overcame him, or God the Holy Spirit who restrains him. However, certain angels through God's command to have the power to overcome him.

"And I saw an angel come down from heaven, having the key of the bottomless pit and a great chain in his hand. And he laid hold on the dragon, that old serpent, which is the Devil, and Satan, and bound him a thousand years, And cast him into the bottomless pit, and shut him up, and set a seal upon him, that he should deceive the nations no more, till the thousand years should be fulfilled: and after that he must be loosed a little season" (Revelation 20:1–3).

"*...That he should deceive the nations no more....*" Right now, Satan is deceiving not just *some* people here and there, but *all* the nations. I think it is reasonable to conclude that most of the people of this world have at some point been deceived by Satan, who even attempted to deceive Jesus Christ through bribery during His ministry on earth.

"Again, the devil taketh him up into an exceeding high mountain, and sheweth him all the kingdoms of the world, and the glory of them; And saith unto him, All these things will I give thee, if thou wilt fall down and worship me" (Matthew 4:8–9).

Those who successfully overcome the relentless deception of Satan are those who firmly believe in Jesus Christ's atoning death at Calvary as the exclusive means for their salvation.

I don't know how anything from the Word of God can be any more convincing about this truth than the following passage from the apostle Paul. Keep in mind while reading this that Catholic Tradition and the works of the law are one and the same.

"Knowing that a man is not justified by the works of the law, but by the faith of Jesus Christ, even we have believed in Jesus Christ, that we might be justified by the faith of Christ, and not by the works of the law: for by the works of the law shall no flesh be justified" (Galatians 2:16).

Some of the laws that the Vatican has imposed on Catholics include precepts that were not established until the fourth century or later. They include doctrines, dogmas, papal decrees, and other pronouncements that were not necessary for the salvation of early Christians because these humanly-conceived and imposed laws had not yet come into being.

The early Church Fathers and Christian faithful were saved because they simply and wisely believed only in the Gospel of Jesus Christ. They were saved without infant baptism, Mariology, indulgences, purgatory, saint and image worship, transubstantiation and, perhaps the most objectionable of all to the Father and Son, Catholic Tradition.

Promulgation of this Tradition was adopted at the Council of Trent in 1545. Then, in 1870, the Vatican Council claimed the infallibility of the pope.

Early in this century, the virgin Mary was made "Co-Redeemer" with Jesus by Pope Benedict XV.

Rome, however, has backed away from a recent international grass-roots effort to reinstate a similar proclamation for Mary. Affirmation would be damaging to the church's leadership role in the Ecumenical Movement. Virtually all Protestant denominations would resist aligning themselves with Rome over this issue.

Satan and his allies have armies of very powerful spirit beings who would just love for us to be complacent about our spiritual condition. If we don't accept the truth, we score another victory for Satan and his legions of helpers. Even for those who have accepted Christ as their personal Savior, the struggle continues.

"For we wrestle not against flesh and blood, but against principalities, against powers, against the rulers of the darkness of this world, against spiritual wickedness in high places" (Ephesians 6:12).

This passage explains how the born again Christian can fight against these wicked powers. This prescription is not for everyone. They are weapons only for those who exclusively believe in the simplicity of the Gospel of Jesus Christ. You will find no man-made doctrines. Everything revolves around the truth that is only contained in His Word, never in the precepts of men.

"Wherefore take unto you the whole armour of God, that ye may be able to withstand in the evil day, and having done all, to stand. Stand therefore, having your loins girt about with truth, and having on the breastplate of righteousness; And your feet shod with the preparation of the gospel of peace; Above all, taking the shield of faith, wherewith ye shall be able to quench all the fiery darts of the wicked. And take the helmet of salvation, and the sword of the Spirit, which is the word of God" (Ephesians 6:13–17).

There is nothing contained in that which you have just read, that even slightly suggests the need for Catholic Tradition. We need all the help we can get in our battle against the forces of Satan, but the precepts of men provide no help at all! For the born again Christian, the solution is very simple:

"For sin shall not have dominion over you: for ye are not under the law, but under grace" (Romans 6:14).

If you have not already done so, please accept the Lord Jesus Christ into your heart right now as personal Savior through the prayer of reconciliation found on page 56.

Then you will no longer be under the Law, but under grace. Only the grace of God can save you! The works of the Catholic Church cannot save you! They never could and they never will!

Chapter 21

Satan Inside The Vatican

'Now I confidently say that whoever calls himself, or desires to be called, Universal Priest, is in his elation the precursor of Antichrist, because he proudly puts himself above all others. Nor is it by dissimilar pride that he is led into error; for, as that perverse one wishes to appear as God above all men, so whoever this one is who covets being called sole priest, he extols himself above all other priests...Certainly Peter, the first of the apostles, himself a member of the holy and universal Church, Paul, Andrew, John - what were they but heads of particular communities? And yet all were members under one Head. And (to bind all together in a short girth of speech) the saints before the law, the saints under the law, the saints under grace, all these making up the Lord's Body, were constituted as members of the Church, and not one of them has wished himself to be called universal. Now let your holiness acknowledge to what extent you swell within yourself in desiring to be called by that name by which no one presumed to be called who was truly holy.'

Pope Gregory the Great (590-604 A.D.)

"And hath made us kings and priests unto God and his Father; to him be glory and dominion for ever and ever Amen."

Revelation 1:6

In November 1996, Rome's largest daily newspaper, *Il Messaggero* reported Satan worship by Catholic Church leaders. The July/August, 1997 *Proclaiming The Gospel*, Vol. 6, No. 4, newsletter provides us with some of the content of the Italian newspaper's coverage. The explosive disclosure was released by Archbishop Emmanual Milingo.

The archbishop charged that members of the Catholic Church hierarchy in Rome are secretly involved in formal satanic worship. Incredibly, he stated this while addressing an international audience of bishops, priests, nuns and laity.

The archbishop went on to say:

> "The devil in the Catholic Church is so protected now that
> he is like an animal protected by the government; put on
> a game preserve that outlaws anyone, especially hunters
> from trying to capture or kill it."[1]

To the question, "Are there men of the curia who are followers of Satan?" Milingo responded, "Certainly there are priests and bishops. I stop at this level of ecclesiastical hierarchy because I am an archbishop; higher than this I cannot go."

In another publication, *Il Tempo*, Milingo cited papal statements to back up his charges.

> "Paul VI said that the smoke of Satan had entered into the
> Vatican, but I have not heard that anyone has seen him
> leave. We must pray so that he will go away."[2]

The name "Satan" means "adversary." In fact, *Webster's Dictionary* provides this definition for Satan:

"The adversary of God and lord of evil in Judaism and Christianity."

One might stop short and associate the designation of God with the Father only. Catholicism rightfully establishes Jesus Christ as God, as the Catechism underscores the importance of Christ throughout its entirety. That is accurate and there is certainly no argument with this.

But the question must be: If Jesus Christ is the central Being of Catholicism, how then can the adversary of Jesus Christ (Satan) be venerated by some of Catholicism's leadership, particularly when done so in the church's worldwide seat of power?

The Catholic Church has become corrupted over the centuries by some of the seemingly ever-present Vatican leadership, in allegiance with the dark spiritual powers found in Ephesians 6:12.

Historians who have chronicled this sordid past find it difficult to get their works published and virtually impossible to get their work displayed in book stores. The Catholic Church has had a great deal of success in squashing the truth. Wouldn't "Satan Worship In The Vatican" be a hot story for CBS to cover in a "60 Minutes" segment? But it is not likely to happen!

Satan attempted to corrupt Christ's own ministry while He was on earth as He prepared to take away our sins. But Satan lost that match of wills. Jesus admonished Satan by saying we must not rely on his bribes but on the Word of God:

"And when the tempter came to him, he said, If thou be the Son of God, command that these stones be made bread. But he answered and said, It is written, Man shall not live by bread alone, but by every word that proceedeth out of the mouth of God" (Matthew 4:3–4).

Although Satan has subsequently won many victories in the Vatican, we can be assured that the simple Gospel of Jesus Christ can set us free from that kind of bondage:

"...If ye continue in my word, then are ye my disciples indeed; And ye shall know the truth, and the truth shall make you free" (John 8:31–32).

"And this is the will of him that sent me, that every one which seeth the Son, and believeth on him, may have everlasting life: and I will raise him up at the last day" (John 6:40).

[1]*Proclaiming The Gospel*, Mike Gendron, July/August, 1997, p.6. Box 940871, Plano, TX
[2]IBID

Chapter 22

Simple Faith

If anyone says that justifying faith is nothing else than confidence in divine mercy which remits sins for Christ's sake, or that it is the confidence alone that justifies us - let him be anathema.

Council of Trent - Canon 12

"Verily, verily, I say unto you, He that heareth my word, and believeth on him that sent me, hath everlasting life, and shall not come into condemnation; but is passed from death unto life."

John 5:24

The word "faith" appears 245 times in the Bible. Faith in Christ is the foundation of the New Testament message. We can be saved from sin only one way: through a firm belief that Jesus Christ died for our sins, rose on the third day and sits at the right hand of God the Father.

We must accept the fact that Jesus' voluntary and substitutionary death on our behalf is a gift. We can do absolutely nothing to merit our own salvation. We must have a simple faith in the belief that Jesus Christ can save us.

We use the word "simple" because nothing else is required; no theological additions are necessary to facilitate our salvation. The Gospel of Jesus Christ is indeed very simple although some theologians want to make it complicated.

"Being justified freely by his grace through the redemption that is in Christ Jesus: Whom God hath set forth to be a propitiation through faith in his blood, to declare his righteousness for the remission of sins that are past, through the forbearance of God" (Romans 3:24 –25).

The Old Testament details a history of the Jews' inability to gain freedom from their sins by keeping the Mosaic Law, the laws provided to them through Moses. After God proved once and for all that man cannot be saved by trying to keep His laws, He gave mankind the greatest gift imaginable; the Gospel, which means "the Good News."

Throughout the New Testament, the Holy Spirit inspired its authors to declare in essense: "Repent of your sins, and believe in Jesus Christ as your personal Savior. Surrender your mind and heart to Him. If you do, you will be saved!"

Historians verify that early Christians believed in this simple faith: They were saved by the New Covenant, the Good News, the Gospel of Jesus Christ. The Good News is that we no longer need to worry about religious laws to assure our salvation.

Rather, God has promised salvation as a gift to all who believe in His Son's atoning sacrifice at Calvary and who live in faith that His sacrifice is sufficient for salvation. For approximately the first 400 years of the Church, most Christians believed this simple message.

When Emperor Constantine became a Christian in A.D. 313 and eventually its defacto head, the dreaded co-mingling of church and state became a way of life. The church and the Roman Empire merged into a single entity. It also established the basis for the Roman Catholic Church as we know it today.

Our search for the truth is to determine Christ's true intentions for His Church. His Church was never intended to be an institution of authority over the believer; rather, it was intended as a Body of believers who, as a unit, would study and abide by His Word.

Most associate the word "church" with a building or a place where crowds of people gather to worship God. But Jesus' definition is quite different. He said: *"For where two or three are gathered together in my name, there am I in the midst of them"* (Matthew 18:20).

How wonderful! Jesus, the Son of God, my personal Savior and Lord, promises to be with me and another believer if we meet in one of our houses to share His Word. We don't have to go to a specified building. His Church is an organism rather than an organization.

My fellow believer and I are there with Jesus by the Holy Spirit's empowering us with a simple faith. We understand beyond a shadow of a doubt that Jesus alone saved us from our sins; past, present and future. His Word is eternal; it never changes. *"Heaven and earth shall pass away, but my words shall not pass away"* (Matthew 24:35).

Here are six additional descriptions of simple faith, assurances of salvation by a belief in the Gospel of Jesus Christ.

1) *"But if we walk in the light, as he is in the light, we have fellowship one with another, and the blood of Jesus Christ his Son cleanseth us from all sin"* (1st John 1:7).
2) *"He that believeth on him is not condemned: but he that believeth not is condemned already, because he hath not believed in the name of the only begotten Son of God"* (John 3:18).
3) *"For I am not ashamed of the gospel of Christ: for it is the power of God unto salvation to every one that believeth; to the Jew first, and also to the Greek"* (Romans 1:16).
4) *"For therein is the righteousness of God revealed from faith to faith: as it is written, The just shall live by faith"* (Romans 1:17).
5) *"For God so loved the world, that he gave his only begotten Son, that whosoever believeth in him should not perish, but have everlasting life"* (John 3:16).
6) *"In whom ye also trusted, after that ye heard the word of truth, the gospel of your salvation: in whom also after that ye believed, ye were sealed with that holy Spirit of promise"* (Ephesians 1:13).

Chapter 23

Diabolical Past

Only faith can recognize that the Church possesses these properties [one, holy, catholic, apostolic] from her divine source. But their historical manifestations are signs that also speak clearly to human reason. As the First Vatican Council noted, the "Church herself, with her marvelous propogation, eminent holiness, and inexhaustible fruitfulness in everything good, her catholic unity and invincible stability, is a great and perpetual motive of credibility and an irrefutable witness of her divine mission."

The Catechism of the Catholic Church - 812

"...That he might sanctify and cleanse it with the washing of water by the word, That he might present it to himself a glorious church, not having spot, or wrinkle, or any such thing; but that it should be holy and without blemish."

Ephesians 5:26-27

Many, including myself, grew up in devout Catholic homes, churches, and schools, and remember fondly the kind and sincere priests, nuns and scores of wonderful Catholic friends and acquaintances.

My first jolt that there might be something wrong in Camelot came at my pre-Cana wedding conference. The young firebrand priest who was counseling us informed my fianceé and me and everyone else in the room: "You can be sure that the Catholic Church is the one true church by the fact that it has survived in spite of its nefarious past."

Having gone through eight years of Catholic grammar school and four years of Catholic high school, my reaction was, "What is he saying?"

My bride-to-be, who was willing to convert to Catholicism at my behest, was also shocked:

"What is this all about?"

Everyone in the room gasped as he laid out a few of the mind-numbing details.

Well, his comments were child's play in comparison to what we find when studying the history of the Church of Rome. My own experience has shown me that many Catholics believe that the work of historians is fiction. It is not! The subject would not even have occurred to me had I not attended these pre-Cana conferences.

The church's disturbing history is accurately recorded by many unbiased historians. However, most Catholics go through life without learning even a hint of the unsavory past of their church.

What purpose does uncovering the past serve? Some Catholics might insist that we would all do better to concern ourselves with contemporary problems and strive to do better in the future. That opinion may seem valid, but its not helpful in this instance. The character of the church

is much the same today as it was in the past. Only circumstances have changed.

Instant global media coverage prevents a contemporary
Vatican from getting away with the outrageous conduct it
has manifested throughout the centuries. Rome can no
longer be in the bloody business of crowning and
dethroning kings and queens, can no longer mass murder
those refusing to kneel to its authority, can no longer
openly condone its leadership's involvement with prostitutes and can no longer sell church offices and titles to the
highest bidder.

So currently, Rome's focus is on the deceptively tame
Ecumenical Movement. The pope wants to be in charge of
the emerging one-world religion. Heading the global
church, however, is just a stepping stone toward accumu-
lating greater world-wide political power.

As indicated earlier, many Bible commentators, as well
as this writer, believe that the false prophet of the last days
will be a pope, the head of the politically correct universal church. As such, he will be the right-hand man to the
coming global dictator, the Antichrist.

As we discussed, many also predict that the much
expanded and governmentally powerful Church of Rome
will turn out to be the great harlot found in the book of
Revelation.

At this point we must scripturally identify this "MYS-
TERY, BABYLON THE GREAT, THE MOTHER OF
HARLOTS AND ABOMINATIONS OF THE EARTH."
Scripture gives us a clear three-fold criteria to identify her:

1) *"And I saw the woman drunken with the blood of the
saints, and with the blood of the martyrs of Jesus: and
when I saw her, I wondered with great admiration"*
(Revelation 17:6).

No one can qualify for the abominable title, "Mystery Babylon," unless she is responsible for the blood of the martyrs of Jesus. Thus the question, "Who is this woman?"

The answer is found in verse 18, *"And the woman which thou sawest is that great city, which reigneth over the kings of the earth."*

2) *"And here is the mind which hath wisdom. The seven heads are seven mountains, on which the woman sitteth"* (Revelation 17:9).

The woman is the city; the city is built on seven hills, and in that city, the blood of the martyrs of Jesus was shed.

3) *"For all nations have drunk of the wine of the wrath of her fornication, and the kings of the earth have committed fornication with her, and the merchants of the earth are waxed rich through the abundance of her delicacies"* (Revelation 18:3).

No city on the face of the earth is so widely known for being as religious a city as "the eternal city of Rome."

Simultaneously, Rome is a political city known as the Vatican, which is recognized by the United Nations. The world's leading religious entity, also the Vatican, has diplomatic relationships with virtually all nations on the earth.

"And there appeared a great wonder in heaven; a woman clothed with the sun, and the moon under her feet, and upon her head a crown of twelve stars: And she being with child cried, travailing in birth, and pained to be delivered" (Revelation 12:1–2).

Satan, the "prince of this world"—or more aptly "the god of this world" as found in certain translations—in many instances has deceived individuals. Has he deceived the leadership of the Vatican, not only throughout the centuries, but to this very day? I don't think that there can be any question about it!

It was not in centuries past that the Vatican distorted God's Ten Commandments; it was in 1994 when *The Catechism of the Catholic Church* effectively eliminated the second commandment. However, this self-proclaimed license to alter God's Word runs shallow in comparison to the antics of Pope Sixtus V.

Sixtus V, the reigning pope in A.D. 1585–1590, embarrassed the Catholic clergy and faithful of his day by rewriting the entire Latin version of the Bible.

Fortunately for the church, Sixtus V lived in the fifteenth century when mass communication and media were nonexistent.

If the current pope were to rewrite the entire Bible today, most of the faithful might just stop being faithful and leave the church, particularly since the Catechism declares:

> "...the books of Scripture firmly, faithfully, and without error
> teach that truth which God, for the sake of our salvation,
> wished to see we confided to the Sacred Scriptures"
>
> —*Catechism of the Catholic Church,* 1994. #107, p. 31.

Of course, Pope Sixtus V didn't know about the 1994 Catechism when he rewrote Sacred Scripture. Fortunately for the Vatican, Pope Sixtus V died a short time after altering the Word of God.

This, of course, provided the Vatican with an opportunity to exercise some damage control. Actually it did a masterful job of masking the truth. In secrecy, a task force of scholars, under the direction of Cardinal Bellarmine, returned the Bible to its near-original Latin form.

Most such historical accounts of the Catholic Church's reprehensible past can be proven, as is the case with the folly of Sixtus V. The Vatican launched a seek-and-destroy mission with respect to the rewritten Bibles, but not all were found and destroyed. In fact one is exhibited in the Bodleian Library in Oxford, England!

With all this firmly in mind, consider author Dave Hunt's comments about this episode:

> "Pope Sixtus V, in a Papal Bull, Aeternus Ille (an allegedly infallible declaration on faith and morals to the entire church), he declared by 'fullness of apostolical power' that this new 'translation' of the Bible must be 'received and held as true, lawful, authentic and unquestioned in all public and private discussions, readings, preachings and explanations.' Anyone who disobeyed was to be excommunicated."[1]

The words of the Vatican, the precepts of men, continuously change, *"But the word of the Lord endureth for ever..."* (1st Peter 1:25).

[1]Aeternus Ille, Papal Bull, as quoted in Dave Hunt's, *A Woman Rides The Beast*, Harvest House Publishers, Eugene, OR, 1994. p.510

Chapter 24

Prostitutes In The Vatican

All the ordained ministers of the Latin Church, with the exception of permanent deacons, are normally chosen from among men of faith who live a celibate life and who intend to remain *celibate* "for the sake of the kingdom of heaven." Called to consecrate themselves with undivided heart to the Lord and to "the affairs of the Lord," they give themselves entirely to God and to men. Celibacy is a sign of this new life to the service of which the Church's minister is consecrated; accepted with a joyous heart celibacy radiantly proclaims the Reign of God.

The Catechism of the Catholic Church - 1579

"I say therefore to the unmarried and widows, It is good for them if they abide even as I. But if they cannot contain, let them marry: for it is better to marry than to burn."

1ˢᵗ Corinthians 7:8-9

I am not placing this chapter in the book to be vicious or gleefully exhibit the dirty laundry of the past. Rather, I consider it necessary to include this chapter to illustrate that when we speak of the Catholic hierarchy, we speak of a man-made organization, (as, incidentally, all churches are,) which is therefore subject to the most horrendous and reprehensible sins. This discussion serves to reinforce the fact that there is no such thing as human organizational infallibility.

At this point, I want to reiterate that the Church of Jesus Christ consists of all born again believers who may be found wherever the Word of God is proclaimed.

The previous chapter alluded to church leaders who were companions of prostitutes. When discussing issues like this with Catholic friends, I often get responses like:

"Now you've gone too far: How can you believe such garbage?"

"Revelations like that are untrue and you know it!"

"Oh! Maybe on a rare occasion such things might have happened, but why make it an issue?"

Good, intelligent people often react in shock. They just don't have a clue as to the facts.

The modern-day Catholic Church faces monumental problems due to the epidemic sexual misconduct by parish priests and other Catholic officials! This, however, is mild when compared to the misbehavior of the Catholic hierarchy of years past. Most Catholics are aware of the former, not the latter, and they opt to stick their heads in the sand with respect to both.

Authors and other commentators point to a long history of prolific bastard infestation within the Vatican. That description shouldn't be shocking because it's simply a factual statement.

Early Catholic Church history portrays priesthood as a role and title that was passed along from father to son. This system of hereditary privilege was even practiced in the highest office of the Catholic Church.

One historian relates that Pope Sylverius (536–537) was fathered by Pope Hormisdas (514–523), and John XI (931–935) by Sergius III (904–911) by his favorite mistress, Marozia.[1]

Among the other bastards who ruled the church were Pope Boniface I (414–422), Gelasius (492–496), Agapitis (535–536), and Theodore (642–649). Adrian IV (1154–1159) was the son of a priest.

No wonder Pope Pius II (1458–1464) said Rome was "the only city run by bastards." Pius himself admitted to fathering at least two illegitimate children by different women, one of whom was married at the time. The rule of celibacy created a market for prostitutes, making Rome the "Mother of Harlots," as forseen by the apostle John.[2]

Visiting Germany in the eighth century, St. Boniface found that none of the clergy honored their vows of celibacy. He wrote to Pope Zachary (741–752):

> "Young men who spent their youth in rape and adultery were rising in the ranks of the clergy. They were spending nights in bed, with four or five women, then getting up in the morning to celebrate mass." Bishop Rathurio complained that if he excommunicated unchaste priests, 'there would be none left to administer the sacraments, except boys.' If he excluded bastards, as canon law demanded, not even boys would be left."[3]

The old adage, "Do as I say, not as I do" certainly applies to the early history of the Vatican. However, the philosophy of dictating to the faithful and then compromising those dic-

tums themselves had been just a sampling of the self-serving posture of the Catholic leadership — not just during the
early times but throughout church history to this very day.

[1]Dave Hunt, *A Woman Rides The Beast*, Harvest House, Eugene,
OR, 1994. p.164–165
[2]IBID
[3]IBID

Chapter 25

Common Sense vs. Infallibility

The supreme degree of participation in the authority of Christ is ensured by the charism of *infallibility*. This infallibility extends as far as does the deposit of divine Revelation; it also extends to all those elements of doctrine, including morals, without which the saving truths of the faith cannot be preserved, explained, or observed.

The Catechism of the Catholic Church - 2035

"Ye also, as lively stones, are built up a spiritual house, an holy priesthood, to offer up spiritual sacrifices, acceptable to God by Jesus Christ."

1ˢᵗ Peter 2:5

Catholic doctrine cannot stand as infallible when judged under the scrutiny of common sense.

Since the 18th century, popes have officially claimed infallibility in all matters of faith and morals. Previously, popes had essentially claimed the same powers of authority and acted accordingly.

Common sense, however, strips away all pretensions that this power was handed down from God because nothing in all of Holy Scripture suggests a need for a transfer of governance from the Father to an earthly religious leader.

The Catechism of the Catholic Church claims Scripture to be "without error." (p.31 #107). Consequently, Catholic history, Tradition, and its current statements are locked in irreconcilable conflict!

Additionally, Holy Scripture certainly does not proclaim the need for a ponderous hierarchical structure found in the Church of Rome.

"Almighty" as in "Almighty God" means exactly that: Almighty God. He has not relinquished any of His rights of governance over our lives! He has never directed through Scripture any transfer of His exclusive authority over our lives to earthly leaders.

Through His Holy Spirit, God gave His prophets knowledge of the future, and the apostles the inspiration to write the one and only instruction book, the Bible. However, nothing written establishes that institutions, or Vicars of Christ, are to rule over our lives.

Documented history continuously challenges our common sense regarding the infallibility of popes. For example, consider the practice of simony, the buying or selling of a church office or ecclesiastical preference, and three simultaneously reigning and allegedly "infallible" popes. Historians relate that simony was a common practice among the members of the early church hierarchy. For example,

Julius II (1503–1513) successfully purchased the highest office of all, that of pope.

An uncontrolled, unchecked, and imbedded practice of simony confronted Pope Urban VI when he took office in 1378. He was challenged with the obvious need to clean house.

Unlike other popes of this nefarious era, he decided to revamp the College of Cardinals as most, if not all, of the sitting "princes of the church" had purchased the title, status, and function of their office.

And let it not be unsaid, "For every buyer there must be a seller." Fortunately for the "princes," they saw the axe coming so they promptly elected another "representative of God on earth," Clement VII, a fellow cardinal, who would be more sympathetic with regard to their status. Back-room politics are not exclusive to our generation.

In 1409 there were still two pretenders, but now with different names, Gregory XII and Benedict XIII. Both claimed to be the Vicar of Christ, so a synod was called to settle the matter. This turned out to be a surprisingly simple matter: The two reigning popes were labeled as "heretics." This was followed by the election of Alexander V, the new and only "legitimate" pope. However, neither of the two incumbents wanted to throw in the towel. Three duly elected popes ruled simultaneously! Unprecedented? Not so! A similar triad of popes had ruled "the one true church" 350 years earlier.[1]

Interestingly, the Latin translation of the Greek word meaning "anti" is "vicarious," which produces the word "vicar." Thus, the Vicar of Christ can be translated as "Antichrist."

How can men like these, their predecessors, and subsequent pretenders, with all their discreditable, harsh, mocking antics declare themselves infallible?

Even worse is they claim lordship over every Catholic's life and have placed every Catholic believer into a system of bondage never intended by God.

The saddest factor of all: Rome is leading a billion followers away from salvation. Few Catholics can declare that they have eternal security based on the documentation we have presented throughout this book. Only the born again Christian can be assured of eternal security, a claim guaranteed by the Word of God and not based on the doctrines of men.

[1]From the historians J.H. Ignas Von Dollinger and Peter DeRosa, various references.

Chapter 26

Common Sense vs. Indulgences and Purgatory

"An indulgence is a remission before God of the temporal punishment due to sins whose guilt has already been forgiven, which the faithful Christian who is duly disposed gains under certain prescribed conditions through the action of the Church which, as the minister of redemption, dispenses and applies with authority the treasury of the satisfactions of Christ and the saints." "An indulgence is partial or plenary according as it removes either part or all of the temporal punishment due to sin." Indulgences may be applied to the living or the dead.

The Catechism of the Catholic Church - 1471

"But Peter said unto him, Thy money perish with thee, because thou hast thought that the gift of God may be purchased with money."

Acts 8:20

"As soon as the coin in the coffer rings, a soul from purgatory springs!"

—Tetzel

Johann Tetzel was a 16th-century authorized Catholic salesman of indulgences, and the above is how he advertised his
services. One thousand years had passed since the death of
Christ before the Catholic Church came up with the concept
of indulgences. Then it took more than 400 years for the
concept of purgatory to be elevated from doctrine to dogma
status at the Council of Florence in 1438.

How did all of the earlier Catholics gain salvation without indulgences? Neither indulgences nor purgatory had yet
been invented. Indulgences, which can simply be classified
as works, are often purchased for cash — which is just
another insult to the Son of God.

All those who have received Jesus Christ as personal
Savior have received complete and full remission of their
sins as a free gift which cannot be purchased at any price.

*"But to him that worketh not, but believeth on him that
justifieth the ungodly, his faith is counted for righteousness"*
(Romans 4:5).

*"Not by works of righteousness which we have done, but
according to his mercy he saved us, by the washing of regeneration and renewing of the Holy Ghost"* (Titus 3:5).

*"For by grace are ye saved through faith; and that not of
yourselves: it is the gift of God: Not of works, lest any man
should boast"* (Ephesians 2:8–9).

The Catholic Church proclaims that works are required to
obtain salvation. Catholics need the seven sacraments and
indulgences that most often require paying money, otherwise they can't get out of purgatory.

According to an apparent gap in Catholic dogma, not a
single Catholic, not even the pope, nor any of the cardinals,

bishops or priests know for certain whether they are saved. The Vatican has never established just how many indulgences are necessary to be released from purgatory. As already mentioned, there are some born again Christians in the Catholic Church, but they have not been justified by the Catholic system. Rather, their acceptance of Jesus Christ's death on their behalf is the exclusive reason for their salvation.

Chapter 27

Peter the Rock: The First Pope? Complicating Simplicity

In order that the episcopate itself might be one and undivided, He placed blesssed Peter over the other apostles, and instituted in him a permanent and visible source and foundation of unity of faith and fellowship. And all this teaching about the institution, the perpetuity, the force and reason for the sacred primacy of the Roman Pontiff and his infallible teaching authority, this sacred synod again proposes to be firmly believed by all the faithful.

Second Vatican Council

If anyone, therefore, shall say that blessed Peter the Apostle was not appointed the Prince of all the Apostles and the visible Head of the whole Church Militant; or that the same directly and immediately received from our Lord Jesus Christ a primacy of honor only, and not of true and proper jurisdiction: let him be anathema.

Council of Trent

"And are built upon the foundation of the apostles and prophets, Jesus Christ himself being the chief cornerstone."

Ephesians 2:20

"And Simon Peter answered and said, Thou art the Christ, the Son of the living God. And Jesus answered and said unto him, Blessed art thou, Simon Barjona: for flesh and blood hath not revealed it unto thee, but my Father which is in heaven. And I say also unto thee, That thou art Peter, and upon this rock I will build my church; and the gates of hell shall not prevail against it" (Matthew 16:16–18).

The Gospel of Jesus Christ, the New Covenant between God the Father and a lost mankind, is made both beautiful and effective through the essence of simplicity.

Remember that the apostles—including Peter—were Jews. By means of Pharisaical influence, and to a lesser degree the Sadducees, a burdensome expansion of God's laws were created. They invented a system of religious bondage by adding an endless list of humanly-conceived regulations to the base of God's Laws, a system which consists of a lot more than just the Ten Commandments. The entire book of Leviticus is devoted to the Law.

This is strikingly similar to Catholic Tradition, a compilation of Catholic laws. The Code of Canon Law of the Catholic Church contains 1752 individual laws and approximately 1631 pages of information.

On the other hand, the New Covenant from the Father to you and me, through His Son, is expressed simply, without endless explanations and burdensome laws. I'll do my best to provide the essential message: Believe in the gift of Jesus Christ's substitutionary and all-atoning death in payment of your sin debt. Have complete faith that Christ's work at Calvary is full and complete. You can add nothing to merit your own salvation.

My point: Like the New Covenant, Matthew 16:16–18, containing a dialogue between Christ and Peter, is nothing more than a simple message. It is not a command to establish a human head of the Christian Church. If it were, it would be similar to another verse in Matthew:

"And Jesus came and spake unto them, saying, All power is given unto me in heaven and in earth. Go ye therefore, and teach all nations, baptizing them in the name of the Father, and of the Son, and of the Holy Ghost" (Matthew 28:18–19).

Notice the phrase: *"All power is given unto me in heaven and in earth."* The words "all" and "me" are critical. If Jesus Christ had desired to give some of His authority to an earthly head of His Church, wouldn't He have said so?

And unlike the command, *"Go ye therefore...,"* no command in Matthew 16:16–18 indicates that the Church would be built upon Peter's authority. Rather, the meaning of the word "rock" in this instance is "a rock of faith."

"...Upon this rock I will build my church." The Greek word for Peter is "petros" meaning "a stone." The Greek word for rock is "petra" meaning "a very large rock or bedrock." Translation: On this stone, I will build my Church. It is doubtful at best, that the Lord intended to build His Church (a big rock) on Peter (a stone).

As you will see, Jesus is twice referred to in Scripture as the "Rock." Moses, the author of Deuteronomy said:

"Because I will publish the name of the LORD: ascribe ye greatness unto our God. He is the Rock, his work is perfect: for all his ways are judgment: a God of truth and without iniquity, just and right is he" (Deuteronomy 32:3–4).

"For who is God save the LORD? or who is a rock save our God?" (Psalm 18:31).

Because of the sensitivity of this subject and its cardinal importance, let us look again at the Scripture in question. The Lord Jesus Himself asked His disciples, *"...But whom say ye that I am?"* (Matthew 16:15).

Now comes the reply, *"And Simon Peter answered and said, Thou art the Christ, the Son of the living God"* (verse 16).

The next verse explains, *"And Jesus answered and said unto him, Blessed art thou, Simon Barjona: for flesh and blood hath not revealed it unto thee, but my Father which is in heaven"* (verse 17).

Thereby, Jesus clearly revealed that the statement Simon Peter made came from *"...my Father which is in heaven."* The words Peter spoke were the words of God which came down from heaven.

Jesus continued, *"And I say also unto thee, That thou art Peter, and upon this rock I will build my church; and the gates of hell shall not prevail against it"* (verse 18). Thus, we clearly see that the Word of God is not built upon "flesh and blood," neither upon the man Peter, but *"...upon this rock."* Which rock? The living Word of God!

This eternal Rock, the Word of God, is further identified in 1st Corinthians 10:4, *"And did all drink the same spiritual drink: for they drank of that spiritual Rock that followed them: and that Rock was Christ."*

Based on these indisputable biblical facts—that His Church will be built upon His Word—Jesus revealed to Peter that he would be the key person through which the Lord would manifest the building of His Church, *"And I will give unto thee the keys of the kingdom of heaven: and whatsoever thou shalt bind on earth shall be bound in heaven: and whatsoever thou shalt loose on earth shall be loosed in heaven"* (verse 19).

Peter was the first to give testimony to the Lord's resurrection, *"...he was seen of Cephas, then of the twelve"* (1st Corinthians 15:5).

He was first to preach the Gospel to the Jews, *"But Peter, standing up with the eleven, lifted up his voice, and said* unto them, Ye men of Judaea, and all ye that dwell at Jerusalem, be this known unto you, and hearken to my words" (Acts 2:14).

He was also first to demonstrate the fulfillment of Old Testament prophecies such as healing the lame, "Then Peter said, Silver and gold have I none; but such as I have give I thee: In the name of Jesus Christ of Nazareth rise up and walk" (Acts 3:6).

And again, Peter was first to execute discipline in the Church, "...Ananias, why hath Satan filled thine heart to lie to the Holy Ghost, and to keep back part of the price of the land?...And Ananias hearing these words fell down, and gave up the ghost..." (Acts 5:3,5).

It was Peter who raised the widow from the dead, "...Tabitha, arise. And she opened her eyes: and when she saw Peter, she sat up" (Acts 9:40).

And it was Peter who first preached the Gospel to the Gentiles, "Then Peter opened his mouth, and said, Of a truth I perceive that God is no respecter of persons" (Acts 10:34).

Never, in any instance did Peter claim to have the power by himself; he always grounded his action upon the eternal Rock of salvation, the Word of God.

After the Lord prophesied about Peter and announced that He would suffer and die, but rise again on the third day, Peter revealed himself as a man full of self-esteem, "Then Peter took him, and began to rebuke him, saying, Be it far from thee, Lord: this shall not be unto thee" (Matthew 16:22).

The Lord answered: "...Get thee behind me, Satan: thou art an offence unto me: for thou savourest not the things that be of God, but those that be of men" (verse 23).

No Bible scholar has ever found the slightest indication that Peter was to be a representative of Christ on earth, or that he would subsequently have successors who would ultimately be labeled as popes.

Virtually every respected Bible scholar suggests that to answer a question about one Bible verse, we must search the rest of the Bible for the answer. In doing so, I found that there are two different verses in different books which proclaim God himself as the "Rock."

Peter said, *"Thou art the Christ, the Son of the Living God."* This is revealed to Peter by Christ's Father and upon Peter's faith (rock) Christ will build His Church. If Matthew 16:15–18 was meant to imply that Peter was to be an infallible lord over God's Church with the authority to appoint successors, Jesus Christ, Who is the Rock, would have said exactly that!

Chapter 28

A Room Full of Theologians

"The task of giving an authentic interpretation of the Word of God, whether in its written form or in the form of Tradition, has been entrusted to the living, teaching office of the Church alone. Its authority in this matter is exercised in the name of Jesus Christ." This means that the task of interpretation has been entrusted to the bishops in communion with the successor of Peter, the Bishop of Rome.

The Catechism of the Catholic Church - 85

"...Why do ye also transgress the commandments of God by your tradition?"

Matthew 15:3

Most Catholics have hardly a clue as to the validity of their church's teachings. After more than 50 years as a faithful Catholic lay person, maybe I possess some degree of credibility as a legitimate commentator. Particularly since leaving the church, I have invested great amounts of time comparing the Scriptures with the Catholic Church's teaching about the salvation of souls. As already illustrated, there is tremendous conflict between the two.

My post-Catholic experience is that few Catholic lay persons know how to defend the church's position on these issues.

They almost always vaguely respond, "Well, the church must be right. I really don't know what more I can say."

They usually can't comment because they only know one side of the centuries-old and eternally important debate between Catholics and born again Christians.

Unfortunately many Catholics exhibit only a minimal knowledge of Scripture and have a surprisingly vague grasp as to what their own church is attempting to convey to them.

The majority of Catholics I have known over the years go to church on Sunday and consider that this sacrifice of time makes them square with God, thus they are heaven bound. Scripture does not make any such promise. Jesus Christ's own words leave little doubt as to the irrelevance of this line of thinking.

"Jesus answered and said unto him, Verily, verily, I say unto thee, Except a man be born again, he cannot see the kingdom of God" (John 3:3).

The Catechism of the Catholic Church gives Tradition and the Catholic Magisterium equal footing with Holy Scripture, thereby institutionalizing a triune authority.

But Scripture states:*"Neither is there salvation in any other: for there is none other name under heaven given among men, whereby we must be saved"* (Acts 4:12).

Therefore Scripture stands alone and does not require man-made tradition or a Magesterium.

Where did the revelation come from to give equal authority to Tradition with that of Holy Scripture? Authors and enforcers of such decrees — popes, cardinals, bishops — are merely human beings like you and me. Men, not God, created these offices of authority.

They cannot place themselves into the same classification as the apostles, prophets and other Holy Spirit-inspired authors of Scripture. Paul, Peter, and other authors of the New Testament actually lived with Christ.

My Bible makes clear that there are only 12 apostles. They are called the "apostles of the Lamb." We can see the documentation in the book of Revelation when the new Jerusalem is being revealed as having 12 foundations. The primary characteristic of an apostle is to be called by the Lord Jesus Christ personally, as was the case with the 12 apostles. One had fallen, thus, Saul of Tarsus became an apostle when He met the Lord on this way to Damascus.

In 1st Corinthians 15, the apostle defends the resurrection of Jesus beginning with verse 5 and then in verse 8 he says, *"And last of all he was seen of me also, as of one born out of due time."* Adding men and declaring them to have apostolic authority is foreign to Scripture. It's all self-serving and does not serve the Lord's wishes.

Chapter 29

God's Word vs. Men's Word

Tradition is to be distinguished from the various theological, disciplinary, liturgical, or devotional traditions, born in the local churches over time. These are the particular forms, adapted to different places and times, in which the great Tradition is expressed. **In the light of Tradition, these traditions can be retained, modified or even abandoned under the guidance of the Church's magesterium.**
The Catechism of the Catholic Church - 83

*"Heaven and earth shall pass away: **but my words shall not pass away.**"*

Luke 21:33

The Word of God, Scripture, never changes. *"Heaven and earth shall pass away: but my words shall not pass away"* (Luke 21:33). Portions of Catholic Tradition have often been changed or rescinded.

Catholic Tradition is often used as the source justifying other Tradition. Then, of course, the Vatican claims all Tradition, altered or unaltered, is equal in authority to Holy Scripture. Did you notice that the Catechism even gives Tradition top billing over Scripture?

The Catechism offers justification for Tradition emanating from pronouncements by early Church Fathers such as Augustine, Aquinas, Bernard, Ireneaus, and Jerome, and further justification by the various Councils of the church. At the Councils of Trent, Lyons, Vatican II, etc., justification references are also attributed to the doctrines of the popes, Acts of the Trials of Joan of Arc, and even from prayers of old.

If your reaction is: "It's a self-perpetuating system," you are absolutely right! It's all in the Catechism. Get a copy and read it yourself. However, you will need some fortitude to get through 2,865 individual topics. Its principal compiler of data, Joseph Cardinal Ratzinger, has already written a follow-up book, *Gospel Catechesis Catechism.*

In a commentary about this new work, the Reverend Peter M.J. Stravinskas, Editor of *The Catholic Answer*, made an interesting comment.

> "...The world-wide bestselling catechism has had such a positive response from ordinary Catholics across the globe. But he (Ratzinger) acknowledges that the response of many theologians and professional religionists have been negative toward the Catechism."[1]

My speculation is that most of the negative comments have come from Catholic theologians. If I were one, I would be upset, too. After studying the Catechism at length, I concluded that it really doesn't answer serious questions one might have about the validity of the labyrinth of Catholic faith. Although it does provide scriptural notes, it also uses substantial amounts of Catholic Tradition to justify its own doctrines and impositions upon the faithful. It's a thinly veiled argument of self-perpetuation, preservation and reverence for the Catholic Tradition.

[1]Excerpted from Ignatius Press, 1997 Catalogue, P.O. Box 1339, Fort Collins, CO 80522. p.6

Chapter 30

Seducing the Reformation

An indulgence is obtained through the Church who, by virtue of the power of binding and loosing granted her by Christ Jesus, intervenes in favor of individual Christians and opens for them the treasury of the merits of Christ and the saints to obtain from the Father of mercies the remission of the temporal punishments due for their sins. Thus the Church does not want simply to come to the aid of these Christians, but also to spur them to works of devotion, penance, and charity.

The Catechism of the Catholic Church - 1478
Indulgentiarum doctrina, 5

"But to him that worketh not, but believeth on him that justifieth the ungodly, his faith is counted for righteousness."

Romans 4:5

As already pointed out, Tetzel was a Catholic salesman of indulgences. He was a Dominican Friar commissioned by Pope Leo X to undertake this assignment. I have assumed thus far that most Catholics know that indulgences are designed to reduce the temporal punishment of sin, thereby reducing the sinners' suffering in purgatory.

Pope Gregory I proposed the concept of indulgences in A.D. 593 and then, at the Council of Florence in 1437, a place called purgatory became church doctrine. The selling of indulgences, which has continuously remained a practice in the Church of Rome, has generated billions of dollars for the Vatican treasury.

Author Dave Hunt provides incredible documentation as to the extent to which the precepts of men have corrupted the teachings of the Catholic Church.

Under Pope Leo X (1513–1521) — who cursed and excommunicated Martin Luther — specific prices were published by the Roman Chancery to be paid to the church for absolution for each imaginable crime.

Even murder had its price. For example, a deacon guilty of murder could be absolved for 20 crowns. The "anointed malefactors," as they were called, once pardoned in this way by the church, could not be prosecuted by civil authorities. Leo's sale of salvation was nothing new. Two hundred years earlier, John XXII (1316–1334) had done the same, setting a price for every crime from murder to incest to sodomy. The more Catholics sinned, the richer the church became.[1]

It was primarily because of the nefarious sale of indulgences that Martin Luther led the Reformation. Through his work and the evangelical work of others such as John Wesley, John Knox, and John Calvin, Rome lost much of its interlocking church/state stranglehold over Europe and most of the world.

Luther had long been an exemplary Catholic cleric. But he had increasingly profound doubts about the church's doctrine, which he found to be unbiblical.

The Catholic Church had developed its own gospel, the gospel of men labeled as Catholic Tradition. The Gospel of Jesus Christ was being diminished during a period of growth and power of the church. Historians write that a fellow monk advised Luther, who believed that Scripture stated that salvation was by faith alone, to study the book of Habakkuk, where it was written, *"...the just shall live by his faith"* (Habakkuk 2:4b)

Luther's zeal to reform the apostate church was reinforced by this, and an abundance of confirming verses throughout the Bible, verses which unequivocally state that a person is saved by faith alone.

The battle lines were set: the apostate church vs. the Gospel of Jesus Christ; the precepts of men vs. the Word of God.

The Luther-led Reformation changed history. The intertwined church/state powerhouse was weakened by the "faith alone" preaching of the reformers. Many of them, like Luther, were former Catholic clergymen. The Church of Rome's power to legislate false doctrine upon large members of non-believing Christians and others was substantially weakened.

We are now seeing a reappearance of the Vatican's intention to gain political influence. Its strategy is to take a leadership role in the Ecumenical Movement and to eventually control the politically correct world-wide religion.

The Bible clearly indicates that our generation is about to witness the birth of a single, universally accepted religion. This amalgamation will be intrinsically coupled with the global government.

Look at the recent past: Pope John Paul II has been credited with ending the Cold War. He has publicly apologized to both Jews and Christians for past atrocities committed against them by the Roman Church.

He has held official dialogues with the leaders of every known religious group. He has blessed virtually every professing form of worship except true evangelism.

His church had already anathematized (cursed) evangelicals over 100 times because they believe in the Gospel of Jesus Christ as their exclusive means of salvation.

Incredibly and sadly, some prominent evangelicals in recent years have also been seduced by the Ecumenical Movement. They have sought to establish closer ties with Rome. This exploratory experience has been formally labeled as *E.C.T, Evangelicals and Catholics Together.*

"This people draweth nigh unto me with their mouth, and honoureth me with their lips; but their heart is far from me" (Matthew 15:8–9a).

God has told us everything we need to know in advance:

"But take ye heed: behold, I have foretold you all things" (Mark 13:23).

His Word illustrates that even as you are reading this book, we are racing toward a one-world government, currency, and religion. The religion will likely be some sort of confederation combining elements of Christianity, paganism, Judaism, Islam and everything else that smacks of political correctness.

How about evangelicals? What will happen to them? That totally depends on the timing. Born again believers will be taken out of the world in concert with the beginning of all of these things. That sounds like about now. That is exactly right. Nothing in the Bible states that the evacuation of the Church cannot happen at any moment, *"And now ye know what withholdeth that he might be revealed in his time. For the mystery of iniquity doth already work: only he who now letteth will let, until he be taken out of the way"* (2nd Thessalonians 2:6–7).

According to the Bible, the Antichrist cannot appear, until the Church has been taken, along with the Holy Spirit, to meet the Lord in the air. Subsequently, those not taken will experience the Great Tribulation, a time that includes such massive destruction that God Himself needs to supernaturally intervene.

"And except those days should be shortened, there should no flesh be saved: but for the elect's sake those days shall be shortened" (Matthew 24:22).

So, the big question: "Are those who are taken exclusively born again Christians, or will others be taken with them?" There is a small number of born again Christians in all churches. All those who are raptured will have a cornerstone belief in being saved by faith alone.

"Therefore we conclude that a man is justified by faith without the deeds of the law" (Romans 3:28).

This is what the Word of God prescribes. Salvation is a gift from God to those who believe they have been justified by Christ's substitutionary death. He made us blameless before the Father.

The Vatican prescribes that Christ's death on our behalf is acceptable doctrine, but that Catholics are still not justified for salvation. Catholicism teaches the necessity for continuously striving toward justification through an obedience to Catholic pronouncements. Unfortunately, they can't tell when salvation has been achieved no matter how many works are done or how many indulgences have been stored up.

"These things have I written unto you that believe on the name of the Son of God; that ye may know that ye have eternal life, and that ye may believe on the name of the Son of God" (1st John 5:13).

Catholics are trapped in the bondage of obtaining merit toward salvation by their own efforts. This is not the Gospel of Jesus Christ, which is beautifully expressed with these words,

"For by grace are ye saved through faith; and that not of yourselves: it is the gift of God: Not of works, lest any man should boast" (Ephesians 2:8–9).

Every Catholic who believes in the church's system of salvation should consider this solemn warning,

"But though we, or an angel from heaven, preach any other gospel unto you than that which we have preached unto you, let him be accursed. As we said before, so say I now again, if any man preach any other gospel unto you than that ye have received, let him be accursed" (Galatians 1:8–9).

[1]Dave Hunt, *A Woman Rides The Beast,* Harvest House Publishers, Eugene, OR, 97402, 1994, p.185

Chapter 31

You and I, Triune Entities

The human body shares in the dignity of "the image of God": it is a human body precisely because it is animated by a spiritual soul, and it is the whole human person that is intended to become, in the body of Christ, a temple of the Spirit:

Man, though made up of body and soul, is a unity. Through his very bodily condition he sums up in himself the elements of the material world. Through him they are thus brought to their highest perfection and can raise their voice in praise freely given to the Creator. For this reason man may not despise his bodily life. Rather he is obliged to regard his body as good and to hold it in honor since God has created it and will raise it up on the last day.

The Catechism of the Catholic Church - 364

"That which is born of the flesh is flesh; and that which is born of the Spirit is spirit."

John 3:6

The God of the Bible consists of three individual enti-
ties incorporated into a single Godhead: the Father, the
Son, and the Holy Spirit.

You and I similarly consist of three parts: body, soul
and spirit. In our case, the most important of the three is
the spirit.

When I was conceived, I was conceived from the seed
of my human father, and I was born of my mother. I was
composed of body, soul and spirit; however, due to my
inheritance, I was born spiritually dead in sin.

When I became born again, my spiritual conception
was by God through His Holy Spirit, *"Which were born,
not of blood, nor of the will of the flesh, nor of the will of
man, but of God"* (John 1:13).

At that moment, all my sins; past, present and future,
were absolved by Christ's death and resurrection because
I accepted Jesus Christ's death and resurrection on my
behalf, and He became my personal Savior and the exclusive means for my salvation. You are about to read one of
the most profound verses in the entire Bible:

*"Whosoever is born of God doth not commit sin; for his
seed remaineth in him: and he cannot sin, because he is
born of God"* (1st John 3:9).

It's God's seed from which we are born again. If you
comment, "Well, I know some born again Christians, and
they still sin!" That's a valid observation (and certainly
this writer is living proof of a born again sinner).

Even though I know for sure that I have been born
again, and that I desperately try not to sin, I still cannot
overcome sin. Only Jesus Christ was successful in
remaining completely sinless while on this planet. Every
living born again Christian, just like everybody else, has
a soul and spirit that is trapped in a corruptible human
body, and will continue to sin.

"If we say that we have no sin, we deceive ourselves, and the truth is not in us" (1st John 1:8).

But only born again Christians know that they have become new creatures.

"Therefore, if any man be in Christ, he is a new creature: old things are passed away; behold, all things are become new" (2nd Corinthians 5:17).

"In whom ye also trusted, after that ye heard the word of truth, the gospel of your salvation: in whom also after that ye believed, ye were sealed with that holy Spirit of promise" (Ephesians 1:13).

That Scripture verse perfectly sums up God's intention for us. Not until born again Christians, deceased or living, are raptured, will we escape this human body so bent on sinning.

"For the Lord himself shall descend from heaven with a shout, with the voice of the archangel, and with the trump of God: and the dead in Christ shall rise first: Then we which are alive and remain shall be caught up together with them in the clouds, to meet the Lord in the air: and so shall we ever be with the Lord" (1st Thessalonians 4:16–17).

At that time we will instantly receive a new imperishable body, one just like that of our Savior. Until then, *"This I say then, Walk in the Spirit, and ye shall not fulfil the lust of the flesh"* (Galatians 5:16).

If our spirit is so important, then what about our soul? The soul is the part of the triune man that relates to our earthly existence. When born again Christians are raptured, they are taken to the Judgment Seat of Jesus Christ. This is not a judgment as to whether or not a person is saved as they have already been assured of salvation. All they did that was counter to God's biblical instructions will be discarded as worthless. The apostle Paul describes this process:

"If any man's work shall be burned, he shall suffer loss: but he himself shall be saved; yet so as by fire" (1st Corinthians 3:15).

On the other hand, all that was done according to God's will, rather than for personal satisfaction, will be rewarded. There will be no born again Christians found at the Great White Throne Judgment. That is reserved for those who adopt a false gospel.

All those who are not born again will learn of their fate at the Great White Throne Judgment which will take place after the Millennium. This judgment will determine one's eternal disposition.

Therefore, the difference between the two judgments is that at the Judgment Seat of Christ no born again Christian will be condemned, but at the White Throne Judgment the lost will be condemned for eternity.

Chapter 32

Birth Pangs of the Last Days

Salvation comes from God alone; but because we receive the life of faith through the Church, she is our mother: "We believe the Church as the mother of our new birth, and not in the Church as if she were the author of our salvation." Because she is our mother, she is also our teacher in the faith.

The Catechism of the Catholic Church - 169

"Jesus answered and said unto him, Verily, verily, I say unto thee, Except a man be born again, he cannot see the kingdom of God. Nicodemus saith unto him, How can a man be born when he is old? can he enter the second time into his mother's womb, and be born? Jesus answered, Verily, verily, I say unto thee, Except a man be born of water and of the Spirit, he cannot enter into the kingdom of God. Marvel not that I said unto thee, Ye must be born again."

John 3:3-5, 7

"Being born again, not of corruptible seed, but of incorruptible, by the word of God, which liveth and abideth for ever."

1st Peter 1:23

You and I are living in a singularly perceptible point in history alluded to more in Scripture than any other: the last days. In my opinion, and that of many others, we are witnessing the advent of the end. If you thoroughly read the book of Revelation, your reaction might be: "How can anyone be enthusiastic? The second three and a half years of the tribulation is the most horrific period of all times?"

Christian scholars are enthusiastic about the approaching latter days because they know the evacuation of the Church will take place prior to the tribulation.

I must be careful to reiterate that the Church consists only of born again Christians. As speculated earlier, this will include some Catholics who are born again, but they represent a small portion of the total Catholic population. Also, as previously indicated, most Catholics following a born again experience promptly leave their church and no longer call themselves Catholics!

What will happen to those Catholics who have not been born again, particularly those living during the immediate days ahead when the whole world witnesses the gathering of the Church from earth to heaven? Five verses of Matthew 24 illustrate the conditions and options for those persons.

"Then shall they deliver you up to be afflicted, and shall kill you: and ye shall be hated of all nations for my name's sake. And then shall many be offended, and shall betray one another, and shall hate one another. And many false prophets shall rise, and shall deceive many. And because iniquity shall abound, the love of many shall wax cold. But he that shall endure unto the end, the same shall be saved" (Matthew 24: 9–13).

"But he that shall endure unto the end, the same shall be saved..." My understanding of Scripture, which is

collaborated by most biblical scholars, is that those Catholics who endure to the end, but remain void of a born again experience will not be saved. The next verse reads:

"And this gospel of the kingdom shall be preached in all the world for a witness unto all nations; and then shall the end come" (Matthew 24:14).

Chapter 33

Sqaundering All Hope

"Faith implies assent of the intellect to that which is believed...To believe is an act of the intellect, inasmuch as the will moves it to assent...Now to believe is immediately an act of the intellect, because the object of that act is the true, which pertains properly to the intellect. Consequently, faith, which is the proper principle of that act, must needs reside in the intellect...Now the formal object of faith is the First Truth, as manifested in Holy Writ and the teachings of the Church, which proceeds from the First Truth. Consequently whoever does not adhere, as to an infallible and Divine rule, to the teaching of the Church, which proceeds from the First Truth manifested in Holy Writ, has not the habit of faith, but holds that which is of faith otherwise than by faith...Now it is manifest that he who adheres to the teaching of the Church, as to an infallible rule, assents to whatever the Church teaches; otherwise, if, of the things taught by the Church, he holds what he chooses to hold, and rejects what he chooses to reject, he no longer adheres to the teaching of the Church as to an infallible rule, but to his own will...Faith adheres to all the articles of faith by reason of one mean, viz. on account of the First Truth proposed to us in the Scriptures, according to the teaching of the Church who has the right understanding of them. Hence, whoever abandons this mean is altogether lacking in faith.

Thomas Aquinas on the Roman Catholic teaching on faith

"So then faith cometh by hearing, and hearing by the word of God."

Romans 10:17

This book is really about the subject of deception. Are Catholics being deceived by a world-wide religious system or is it the author who is misguided? One side has to be wrong, as there can be no middle ground.

Catholics are indeed confronting more than just important earthly decisions. These decisions involve all of eternity; their consequences are forever! Perhaps the most often overlooked tragedy of faulty spiritual decisions is that once a person is condemned, his future holds no hope!

If your spiritual choice is wrong, you will surely recall when you turned away someone who tried to witness to you about the truth. I remember one godly commentator expressing his belief that this kind of remembrance results in the most intense form of hellish pain. God provides the unbeliever with one or more opportunities to reverse spiritual decisions which could become eternal errors. Those who choose the wrong path are forever trapped in the abyss with no hope of ever being with God, let alone ever escaping the horrors of hell.

Whatever your decision is, it becomes irreversible; your disposition is final. After a man commits the eternal error prior to death and finds himself existing in a domain of misery, his thoughts will surely turn to what could have been. He could have been in the glory of heaven with the Son of God, who died a horrible death to qualify to be his personal Savior.

The Father gives us free will, and accordingly, we're encumbered with the consequences of our erroneous decisions. When we err, we fall short of the glory of God and are condemned forever with no hope!

I would like you to consider making three decisions, three commitments actually, which can prevent this eternal tragedy.

- Your first decision will be to believe that it can happen to you, but that it can also be avoided.

    "For all have sinned, and come short of the glory of God" (Romans 3:23).

    "For the wages of sin is death; but the gift of God is eternal life through Jesus Christ our Lord" (Romans 6:23).

- Your second decision is to embrace this belief:

God the Father, through the Holy Spirit, guided the apostle Paul to write the above two verses and expects you to believe them and be guided by them. His scriptural proposal (Romans 6:23) is exquisitely easy to adopt and to believe.

However, the Catholic Church has made a counter-proposal, an extremely complex labyrinth of works. Let's compare the two: God's way and the Vatican's way.

God's Way: Sin causes death, whereby your eternity will be void of the presence of God.

To offset this, God offers the free gift of eternal life, in the presence of God, through an exclusive belief in Christ Jesus as your personal Savior.

Vatican's Way: We, too, believe in Jesus Christ, but you also need us, the Catholic Church, to have a chance for salvation.

We have created works that you must perform, otherwise you go to hell!

You must accept the necessity for, and the need to participate in the seven sacraments, including the immolation and transubstantiation of Jesus in the Mass.

You are required to worship Mary and other saints, as Jesus is not sufficient.

You need indulgences to get out of purgatory, but we don't know how many.

You must believe in all of Catholic Tradition, not God's prophets, but rather the precepts of men.

Lastly, you must accept the Magisterium's interpretation of the Bible.

However, the Bible clearly instructs that it is noble-minded to study the Bible on your own!

"Now these were more noble minded than those in Thessalonica, for they received the word with great eagerness, examining the Scriptures daily, to see whether these things were so" (Acts 17:11).

In addition to the Catholic works listed above, there are many others. The Bible, which the Catechism labels as inerrant, relentlessly proclaims that works are not necessary for salvation! Then, on the other hand, with allegedly infallible doctrine, the Vatican proclaims that works are necessary for salvation! I'll venture that less than one percent of the world's one billion Catholics have come to understand this undeniable inconsistency in Catholicism.

• The third and last decision you should make is to accept, once and for all, that Scriptures say what they mean and mean what they say!

If you have trouble understanding a verse, other verses in the Bible will explain its meaning.

When Bible "experts" attempt to allegorize or spiritualize certain verses, they often compromise God's Word.

Virtually every Christian-based theology will agree that the wages of sin is death. But the Catholic Church challenges the next part of Romans 6:23, *"...but the free gift of God is eternal life in Christ Jesus our Lord."*

They challenge the Word of God by declaring that the free gift of God, eternal salvation, by a simple belief in His Son is not enough!

Rome has thought up all types of works throughout the centuries and has added them to God the Father's free gift.

Let's say that you have a problem believing the simplicity of God's way as valid (Romans 6:23). This is certainly understandable because you have been taught about the need for numerous Catholic works throughout your entire life. So let's follow the hallmark belief of Christian Bible scholars.

We'll look for another verse confirming that Romans 6:23 says what it means and means what it says. We don't have to look very far. Confirmation is in the same book of Romans. Catholic theologians have a very difficult time with this verse, but rather than comment further it will be obvious as to why they like to avoid it.

"But to him that worketh not, but believeth on him that justifieth the ungodly, his faith is counted for righteousness" (Romans 4:5).

Please allow me to comment on this verse in order to emphasize its meaning even though it's straightforward and quite easy to understand. Assuming you have done so, I believe that your understanding will be very similar to this:

A person who has not performed works, (such as works prescribed for Catholics) but believes in Jesus Christ as his personal Savior is justified. That person is not saved by works but rather through faith in Jesus Christ as the exclusive justification for salvation. He is reckoned as righteous by His belief in Jesus Christ for salvation.

I am going to ask you, if you have not already done so, to slowly and very sincerely pray the prayer of reconciliation found on page 56.

The next chapter will be very important if you have prayed the prayer of reconciliation and accordingly believe that you are now a born again Christian. You should believe that you have obtained eternal security by repenting of all sin and have accepted Jesus Christ as personal Savior and Lord of your life. Welcome, dear brothers and sisters in Christ, and new sons and daughters of the Father!

But read on; it's very important that you do! There is a way to determine whether or not you have been truly born of the Spirit of God.

Chapter 34

Let's Not Deceive Ourselves

The Council of Trent states: 'If anyone denieth, either that sacramental confession was instituted, or is necessary to salvation, of divine right; **or saith, that the manner of confessing secretly to the priest alone, which the Church hath ever observed from the beginning**, and doth observe, is alien from the institution and command of Christ, and is a human invention: let him be anathema.

The Canons and Decrees of the Council of Trent

"In whom we have redemption through his blood, the forgiveness of sins, according to the riches of his grace...In whom ye also trusted, after that ye heard the word of truth, the gospel of your salvation: in whom also after that ye believed, ye were sealed with that holy Spirit of promise, Which is the earnest of our inheritance until the redemption of the purchased possession, unto the praise of his glory."

Ephesians 1:7, 13-14

There are fraudulent "Christians." Sadly, they come into contact with others to whom they project a false representation of Christianity. Many television evangelists are guilty of this.

Years ago, when I first accepted the Lord, I tried to witness to a Catholic friend who said he wanted to obtain eternal security.

My friend, who was about 80 years old at the time, had a reputation of being self-centered and stubborn. Nevertheless, I had a new zeal for bringing people to the true Gospel of Jesus Christ, so I enthusiastically moved forward.

He and I, and our wives set a dinner date with the understanding that he and I would spend some time alone before leaving for the best restaurant in town — where dinner would be on me.

After much preparation, I went to bat for the Lord. I had previously asked my friend to listen to an audio tape by a respected theologian regarding the eternal disposition of those who were not saved at the time of death. Admittedly, this was a scary subject for anyone. However, this particular tape presented the subject matter in a low-key, dignified and nonintrusive manner.

"Well, how did you like the tape?" I asked him.

"I could only listen to the beginning and then I had to turn it off," he said.

"Can't stand listening to someone telling me that I'll be going to hell. Listen, Dick, I go to mass almost every Sunday and I don't hear anything like that from the priests. Also, you promised me that if I came over here you would show me how I can be assured of salvation. But, I surely don't want to hear any more of that kind of stuff on the tape."

Wow! My first formal presentation of the Word of God to an unsaved person was off to a poor start.

My friend didn't want to hear the Good News of the Gospel of Jesus Christ. He was only interested in a magic formula assuring salvation.

After my presentation and our conversation, we got around to the prayer of reconciliation. I emphasized the absolute need for a repentant heart and the necessity of understanding the meaning of every single world. But, above all, I stressed that he had to have the conviction that what he was saying was the truth from the Word of God. "Yes, yes, I understand that," he said. "Let's get on with it." He recited the prayer out loud.

Although I had my own serious doubts, my friend thought that he was now spiritually secure for all eternity. After our dinner, he continued to go to Mass. Now that's okay, as I already expressed, there are some born again Christians in every church, including the Catholic Church. I was, in fact, one of them! But I don't believe that my friend was one of them. Later, I became convinced that he was still lost because he didn't exhibit the tell-tale signs of a person truly born again of the Spirit of God.

During the years following this incident, I have come to realize certain individuals will not permit God the Father to help them. They refuse to be convicted by the truth of the Holy Spirit. I was new to evangelism and did not yet understand this.

God sends upon them a deluding influence. Most Catholics insist on adhering to the false gospel of Rome, rather than accepting the Gospel of God's Son which requires an exclusive belief in Christ for salvation. It contains no provision for Catholic Tradition.

"And with all deceivableness of unrighteousness in them that perish; because they received not the love of the truth, that they might be saved. And for this cause God shall send

them strong delusion, that they should believe a lie" (2nd Thessalonians 2:10–11).

God knows that those of us who believe we have had a born again experience will want to determine whether or not we are, in fact, born again. The Holy Spirit of God will prompt the true believers to manifest certain characteristics. We will be known by our fruits.

"Every tree that bringeth not forth good fruit is hewn down, and cast into the fire. Wherefore by their fruits ye shall know them" (Matthew 7:19–20).

Those who claim to be born again but are not will be condemned. They will be thrown into the fire. The vast majority of all those who have professed Catholicism as well as other Christians in name only throughout the ages will bemoan this decision at the Great White Throne Judgment.

Remember: All born again Christians will be recompensed for their deeds at the Judgment Seat of Christ. They will not participate in the Great White Throne Judgment. Those Catholics finding themselves condemned will counter God's banishment with numerous appeals: "Didn't I faithfully go to Mass? Didn't I receive all the sacraments? Didn't I worship Mary and the other saints? Didn't I receive many indulgences from my church?"

Millions who have lived throughout the centuries will utter desperate appeals like these, but to no avail.

"Not every one that saith unto me, Lord, Lord, shall enter into the kingdom of heaven; but he that doeth the will of my Father which is in heaven. Many will say to me in that day, Lord, Lord, have we not prophesied in thy name? and in thy name have cast out devils? and in thy name done many wonderful works? And then will I profess unto them, I never knew you: depart from me, ye that work iniquity" (Matthew 7:21–23).

Notice the nature of the appeals. Those who act, look and talk like Christians will rely on such claims. Buddhists, Hindus, Muslims or others won't be taking such a stance, just *counterfeit* Christians.

The book of Galatians contains an abundance of verses pertaining to the fruits of human behavior. We have the "fruits of the flesh" and the "fruits of the Spirit." Born again Christians will exhibit the fruits of the Holy Spirit. Those who continue to exhibit the fruits of the flesh are not likely to have had a genuine conversion experience.

"This I say then, Walk in the Spirit, and ye shall not fulfil the lust of the flesh. For the flesh lusteth against the Spirit, and the Spirit against the flesh: and these are contrary the one to the other: so that ye cannot do the things that ye would. But if ye be led of the Spirit, ye are not under the law" (Galatians 5:16–18).

In the next three verses, the apostle Paul describes the fruits of the flesh. If a person claims to be born again and continues to exhibit these characteristics he or she is likely a born again Christian in name only.

"Now the works of the flesh are manifest, which are these; Adultery, fornication, uncleanness, lasciviousness, Idolatry, witchcraft, hatred, variance, emulations, wrath, strife, seditions, heresies, Envyings, murders, drunkenness, revellings, and such like: of the which I tell you before, as I have also told you in time past, that they which do such things shall not inherit the kingdom of God" (Galatians 5:19–21).

In the next three verses, Paul illustrates the fruits of the Spirit, the Holy Spirit. Those who claim to be born again after coming to Christ with a sincere prayer of reconciliation, and who constantly exhibit these truths are surely saved children of the Father.

"But the fruit of the Spirit is love, joy, peace, long-suffering, gentleness, goodness, faith, Meekness, temperance: against such there is no law. And they that are Christ's have crucified the flesh with the affections and lusts. If we live in the Spirit, let us also walk in the Spirit" (Galatians 5:22–25).

Chapter 35

When Catholics Die

All who die in God's grace and friendship, but still imper-
fectly purified, are indeed assured of their eternal salvation;
but after death they undergo purification, so as to achieve the
holiness necessary to enter the joy of heaven.

The Catechism of the Catholic Church - 1030

*"We are confident, I say, and willing rather to be absent
from the body, and to be present with the Lord."*

2nd Corinthians 5:8

It is necessary to repeat something vitally important to the reader who has petitioned for reconciliation with God, the prayer found on page 56. This is not a magic formula guaranteeing salvation. Rather, it must be predicated on a firm and sincere belief that we cannot be saved by an obedience to humanly-conceived religious doctrines.

The words in the prayer are correct but one's heart must also be genuinely convicted. If you are not sure that you are saved, pray with every ounce of truthfulness you possess to the Father, in Jesus' name, asking Him for the guidance of the Holy Spirit. If, as a result, you are truly convinced of the words in your prayer of reconciliation, then you will surely obtain the peace of heart inherent in knowing that you have eternal security.

Soon after this born again experience, I suggest that you read the first three chapters in the book of Colossians. You will find some glorious verses confirming the wisdom of your decision to believe exclusively in the Word of God, the Holy Bible. Some appropriate passages follow. The Father and His Son, your personal Savior, welcome you, dear brother or sister, to the Body of Christ. Henceforth, you and I will look forward with incredible excitement and enthusiasm for the coming of our Savior!

"Who hath delivered us from the power of darkness, and hath translated us into the kingdom of his dear Son: In whom we have redemption through his blood, even the forgiveness of sins" (Colossians 1:13–14).

"In the body of his flesh through death, to present you holy and unblameable and unreproveable in his sight" (Colossians 1:22).

"Beware lest any man spoil you through philosophy and vain deceit, after the tradition of men, after the rudiments of the world, and not after Christ" (Colossians 2:8).

"And you, being dead in your sins and the uncircumcision of your flesh, hath he quickened together with him, having forgiven you all trespasses; Blotting out the handwriting of ordinances that was against us, which was contrary to us, and took it out of the way, nailing it to his cross" (Colossians 2:13b-14).

"If ye then be risen with Christ, seek those things which are above, where Christ sitteth on the right hand of God. Set your affection on things above, not on things on the earth. For ye are dead, and your life is hid with Christ in God. When Christ, who is our life, shall appear, then shall ye also appear with him in glory" (Colossians 3:1–4).

The book of Colossians couldn't be more persuasive in its message that believing in the Gospel of Jesus Christ is the only means for our salvation.

The apostle Paul also exhorts us not to be deluded by any other message, no matter how persuasive. *"Beware lest any man spoil you through philosophy and vain deceit, after the tradition of men, after the rudiments of the world, and not after Christ"* (Colossians 2:8).

"That their hearts might be comforted, being knit together in love, and unto all riches of the full assurance of understanding, to the acknowledgement of the mystery of God, and of the Father, and of Christ; In whom are hid all the treasures of wisdom and knowledge. And this I say, lest any man should beguile you with enticing words" (Colossians 2:2–4).

Finally, we come full circle to the eternal question by adding two words to the title of this book: *When Catholics Die...*What Happens? I'll repeat the answer given by Jesus Christ Himself:

"Jesus answered and said unto him, Verily, verily, I say unto thee, Except a man be born again, he cannot see the

kingdom of God" (John 3:3). Then, in Romans, the apostle Paul says.

"Therefore being justified by faith, we have peace with God through our Lord Jesus Christ: By whom also we have access by faith into this grace wherein we stand, and rejoice in hope of the glory of God" (Romans 5:1–2).

Chapter 36

EPILOGUE

*"Knowing that Christ being raised from the dead dieth no more; death hath no more dominion over him. For in that he died, he died unto sin **once**: but in that he liveth, he liveth unto God."*

Romans 6:9-10

*"Who needeth not daily, as those high priests, to offer up sacrifice, first for his own sins, and then for the people's: for this he did **once**, when he offered up himself."*

Hebrews 7:27

*"For then must he often have suffered since the foundation of the world: but now **once** in the end of the world hath he appeared to put away sin by the sacrifice of himself."*

Hebrews 9:26

*"So Christ was **once** offered to bear the sins of many; and unto them that look for him shall he appear the second time without sin unto salvation."*

Hebrews 9:28

*"By the which will we are sanctified through the offering of the body of Jesus Christ **once** for all."*

Hebrews 10:10

*"But this man, after he had offered **one** sacrifice for sins for ever, sat down on the right hand of God."*

Hebrews 10:12

I hope these simple words have shown you that there is a contradiction between the things that are being taught in the Catholic Church regarding eternal salvation and that which is clearly taught in the Holy Scriptures.

My only motive for writing this book is for Catholics who are honestly searching for the truth of the Scripture to ask themselves this question before God: "Where will I go when I die?"

It is my hope and prayer, after having read this book, you admit that it is impossible for you to save yourself and that it is equally impossible for the Catholic Church (or any church for that matter) to save you. Then you will be on the right track because Jesus came to save sinners.

The moment you recognize that you are one of them, you may come to Him in simple child-like faith. Then pray the prayer of reconciliation. Once you've done that, thank Him daily that He has saved you for all eternity; thank Him that He has shed His blood for your sins, and thank Him that He has promised to come again!   ■

INDEX

Order Extra Copies of this book for friends, relatives and co-workers.